Clear, Hold, and Build:

The Role of Culture in the Creation of Local Security Forces

A Monograph
by
MAJ Michael R. Evans
Army National Guard of the United States

MENS EST CLAVIS VICTORIAE

School of Advanced Military Studies
United States Army Command and General Staff College
Fort Leavenworth, Kansas

AY 05-06

Abstract

CLEAR, HOLD, AND BUILD: THE ROLE OF CULTURE IN THE CREATION OF LOCAL SECURITY FORCES by MAJ Michael R. Evans, ARNGUS, 64 pages.

In Stability and Reconstruction Operations (SRO), most recently typified by the Global War on Terror (GWOT) the US faces environments that require large and inexpensive forces that can operate effectively in protracted low-intensity environments. The US, however, has developed its land forces so that they are optimized for operational maneuver and deployment from strategic distances, and are therefore small, expensive, fast moving, firepower-intensive, and intended for short-duration engagements that seek to shatter similar enemy formations. The GWOT postulates successive campaigns for the foreseeable future; this requires the disengagement and reconstitution of forces between campaigns. If these campaigns are seen as large scale counter-insurgent "clear and hold" operations, then the counterinsurgent principle of holding cleared areas in order to prevent re-infiltration of enemy forces then becomes a concern. A third component, "build," is necessary to fill the vacuum left when US forces depart. Suitable local security institutions are the key to holding these areas, by sustaining security, allowing the disengagement of US forces for other efforts, and allowing stability to develop without substantial interference.

Construction of such institutions is not without risk. Successful efforts can be built around the development of effective local security, however without culturally acceptable forms of such institutions there is a tendency for them to fail in the absence of their sponsor. Further, some security institutions create an undesired synergy with the negative elements of local cultures, especially in environments that lack the civil infrastructure to restrain them from taking political control. Designing institutions that are not merely culturally acceptable but that are also not culturally disposed to political opportunism and exploitation is a complex task that requires a deep and holistic understanding of the problem and the environment.

This monograph examines this problem from a cultural standpoint, focused on internal security formations that are generally categorized as "constabularies." It does so by defining the environment and problem, examining the historic roles and elements of culture and constabularies, identifying elements common to successful constabularies, and listing cultural principles and elements for planning the establishment of constabularies. It then illustrates these constructs by examining two case studies, Haiti 1915-1934 and Morocco 1907-1919, that were selected for their specific cultural environments. It concludes by summarizing elements that allow constabularies to be successful, principles for the creation of constabularies, and the mitigation of the tendency toward Praetorianism. It concludes by discussing the political mechanism whereby the culturally successful creation and employment of a constabulary benefits sustained SRO such as the GWOT by allowing sustained operations over time at reduced direct political cost to the US or other such intervening powers.

TABLE OF CONTENTS

Introduction

The campaign plan and strategy must be adapted to the character of the people encountered.

United States Marine Corps, *Small Wars Manual 1940*

Preface

A common prerequisite for military planning is to understand the enemy. Knowledge of foreign culture is a key part of this understanding, a part that is more important now than ever. Once it was enough to simply understand how a foreign culture affected the way an enemy army would fight. Today planners must consider how an entire enemy society will react to conflict, to post-conflict effects, and to subsequent efforts (now commonly referred to as Stability and Reconstruction Operations or SRO). The creation of security is one such effort that is dependent on knowledge of foreign culture. This is not merely a matter of understanding the interactions between a military force and a local population; the understanding that is required today goes much deeper because policy decisions that have shaped current US military forces have created a gap. This gap can only be filled by actions that require broad and deep knowledge of local cultures.

The Global War on Terror (GWOT) exposes this gap. US forces are organized, trained, and equipped for high-intensity, short-duration conventional campaigns. They are ill-matched to the low-intensity, long-duration requirements typified by recent SRO campaigns in Afghanistan and Iraq. Even if the US built a capability and sufficient capacity to execute long-term internal security in support of SRO, this would be at odds with the stated US policy of encouraging local participatory governments. The gap, therefore, is that having won an initial series of battles, US forces intend and are designed to quickly depart. A sustained effort is still necessary, however, to re-establish internal security after such a campaign. If the US forces do not intend and are not

1

designed to remain for this effort, then US policy requires that some other force will, preferably a local one that will also contribute to local governance and long term stability.

The Problem

Creating these local forces is more complicated than just issuing weapons and equipment and providing some training, however. This point is illustrated by one of the first efforts in SRO: to construct an effective internal security force. Such a force should function at the interface between military actions (against insurgents) and law enforcement (against criminals.) Further, in some situations crime and insurgency may be indistinguishable. Therefore, such an effort calls for an institution that can function as both military and law enforcement in the local cultural environment. One form of paramilitary police institution is a constabulary, "an armed police force organized on military lines but separate from the regular army."[1]

Constabularies have met with mixed success, however, largely due to lack of understanding of cultural factors on the part of the intervention forces that sponsor them. Constabularies, more so than conventional military forces, act on "cultural terrain."[2] This cultural terrain is a complex system that varies by situation and adapts: what makes a specific solution effective in one place and time may be irrelevant or may even have a negative effect in another.

---

[1] Webster's New Collegiate Dictionary (1981), s.v. "constabulary." Permanent constabulary forces have been considered at various times by the US military but not adopted, generally because they are considered a specialized organization that would have limited applicability elsewhere. Historically the US military has performed such roles, when necessary, with "general purpose forces," regular units detailed to special missions. The small size of the contemporary US military, however, limits the use of this technique for more than short periods.

[2] This is a widely referenced concept that has no standard definition but is generally considered as a sociological construct of the specific factors that affect the thinking and behavior of individuals or groups from a given society. William Wunderle states "Cultural Factors are dynamic aspects of society that have the capacity to affect military operations. They include religion, ethnicity, language, customs, values, practices, perceptions and assumptions, and driving causes like economy and security. All these factors affect the thinking and motivation of the individual or group and make up the cultural terrain of the battlespace." He also provides a graphical representation of his construct for cultural terrain in his work for the RAND Corporation. Wunderle, William, "Through the Lens of Cultural Awareness: Planning Requirements in Wielding the Elements of National Power," unpublished brief presented to the RAND Corporation at the Joint Readiness Training Center, Fort Polk, LA, 2003, slides 16 and 66.

The local culture may change in unanticipated ways once a military intervention affects the social system. The success of creating a constabulary is therefore dependent on understanding the local culture and how specific local cultural issues will affect the process and outcome of that effort. While some tactics that work in one situation may not work in another, nevertheless it should be possible to identify common analytical elements that can be applied across a wide variety of cultures to aid in planning such efforts.

Stability and Reconstruction

SRO, while it is in common use in both the US Department of Defense and the Department of State, is not yet officially defined. Generally, SRO is a form of external intervention that seeks to create, from existing institutions or in entire new forms, local capability and capacity that can function effectively in the absence of external intervention. The intent of SRO is to improve local conditions and forge sustained improvement so that a reconstructed state can function in the international system. As used in SRO, however, the word "reconstruction" can be misleading. Reconstruction may be the rebuilding of physical infrastructure. Reconstruction may also be efforts to change conditions within a society to stabilize that society.

Creating conditions within a society is not a simple task. Society is a complex system of systems that may not be subject to predictable direction, but only to evolutionary "nudges" according to generalized outcomes in an emergent strategy.[3] No society can be perfected; even stable societies suffer internal inefficiencies and conflicts. The act of intervention may produce enormous changes in the system so that prediction of an outcome will be problematic at best. In an emergent strategy understanding the factors that affect the system allows planners and decision-makers to observe causes and effects and modify their decisions accordingly. This cycle

---

[3] An emergent strategy is a technique in which, rather than a single, integrated approach (which assumes perfect realization brought about by perfect foresight, which implied inflexibility of application), consists of actions taken "...one by one, which converged in time in some sort of consistency or pattern... in effect testing the market." See Mintzburg, Henry, *The Rise and Fall of Strategic Planning*. New York: The Free Press, 1994, pages 24-27.

of observation and decision, applied over time as the situation evolves, helps to mitigate risk

through increasing understanding. The SRO planner has to start with a realistic mission and an

effective system of analysis, however, or the initial decisions may doom this effort before it

begins. When planning the creation of a constabulary, analysis according to a common set of

analytical elements that are appropriate to the culture and acceptable to the local populace is

critical to this beginning.

The Security Environment

The GWOT is based on a series of sustained military and non-military efforts to eradicate

the threat posed to the United States by terrorists and their supporters.[4] This is a sustained and

resource-intensive effort, conducted worldwide, and involving large areas and substantial

populations. Current US military doctrine of rapid and decisive operational maneuver from

strategic distance is ill-matched to this effort.[5]

Contemporary US forces can shatter and disrupt enemy conventional forces and occupy

specific objectives. They are, however, unable to occupy large areas for extended periods of time

owing to their need to return home to "reset" for future operations and other requirements. The

rotation of additional US forces into theaters of operation is limited by forces available for such

---

[4] President George Bush, in a speech to the National Endowment for Democracy on 6 October 2005, describes a strategy of four campaigns: preventing future terrorist attacks, denying access to weapons of mass destruction, denying radicals the support of outlaw regimes, and denying militants the control of any nation. Transcript by the White House at
http://www.whitehouse.gov/news/releases/2005/10/20051006-3.html.

[5] Department of Defense, the National Military Strategy, page 7, paragraph II (3) defines the principles whereby US forces are expected to act as agility, decisiveness, and integration and goes on to state that, "These principles *stress speed*, allowing US commanders to exploit an enemy's vulnerabilities, *rapidly seize the initiative and achieve endstates.* They support the concept of surging capabilities from widely dispersed locations to mass effects against an adversary's centers of gravity to achieve objectives." The phrasing is important as it is clearly focused at the operational level, which has to do with achieving objectives that lead to strategic aims. The absence of strategic terminology is noteworthy. (Emphasis in *italics* added by the author.) Andrew Krepinevich uses the term, "... the Army, which had prepared itself to compete as a world-class sprinter, was now being asked to run a marathon." Krepinevich, Andrew, "The Thin Green Line," background paper published by the Center for Strategic and Budgetary Assessment, 14 August 2004.

operations.[6] This creates a dichotomy in which the US can quickly defeat enemy conventional forces, only to face long-term efforts to stabilize regions without sufficient forces in order to prevent the resurgence of enemy opposition.

The GWOT illustrates this dichotomy. In recent years US forces have fought in remote locations, on fractured and poorly understood cultural terrain, and where economic and/or political upheavals are rife. The purpose of these military efforts has been to change the political environment of the region(s). The conventional combat phases of the operations have been quick and lethal, with advanced US or allied forces employing vast technological overmatch to quickly shatter any conventional opposition. The ensuing SRO environment, however, drags on for years. History and the pace of current operations suggest they may last for decades.[7] In such efforts the term "Exit Strategy" does not apply because these conflicts are ultimately political rather than military.[8] The outcome is not the successful military operation, but what form the new political environment will take and how to shape it. Military actions anticipated as short-term operations turn out to be only the opening moves of long-term campaigns.

The US Department of Defense Joint Publication 1-02 describes a campaign as "… a series of related military operations aimed at accomplishing a strategic or operational objective

---

[6] Even given the employment of the Army Reserve and the Army National Guard to their maximum extent, Army forces are stretched to the point where embedded trainers for the Afghan National Army and commanders and staff of Provincial Reconstruction Teams are increasingly being drawn from the US Navy and the US Air Force. Non-Army personnel are now being given 6-7 week pre-deployment training to compensate for their lack of land warfare command and staff skills. Author's discussion with Commander Kimberly Evans, USN, commander PRT-Herat, PRT-Laghman, and FOB-Laghman (Operation Enduring Freedom, 2004-2005) and also with Mr. Les Grau, Foreign Military Studies Office, 21 October 2005.

[7] Senior (2-star and higher) guest speakers at the Command and General Staff College and the School of Advanced Military Studies have unanimously stated that this is "a long war;" some have mentioned estimates of 30 years or more in relation to a "Cold War" like struggle. Author's notes, CGSC and SAMS, Fort Leavenworth, Kansas, Academic Years 2004-2006.

[8] This is arguably true of any campaign; it is more an issue now, however, due to the increasingly indistinct boundary between military and political efforts and due to a global information and economic environment that renders all such efforts local political issues.

within a given time and space."[9] A campaign is a succession of operations or battles that build on

the successes of earlier efforts. In conventional wars this has generally meant a series of battles

designed to wear down an enemy force that re-constitutes itself even as the attacker consolidates

his gains. Actions to shape the environment after the conventional conflict have generally been

regarded as separate and subsequent efforts. Recent campaigns, however, have been against

enemies whose conventional forces are shattered almost immediately or that deliberately avoid

decisive engagement. In these cases the successive operations have been conducted against

insurgencies, as drawn-out attempts to shape a new political environment while simultaneously

isolating small, mobile, and dispersed enemy forces that blend with the local population. This

campaign is the current security problem in SRO.

One principle of such campaigns is to hold areas once they have been cleared of

organized enemy forces in order to prevent the resurgence of enemy forces and to allow follow-

on efforts. These efforts generally include the reconstruction or replacement of the social and

economic institutions of the region in order to shape the new political environment. This new

environment contributes to the isolation of the insurgents from the population that they are

employing as a screen and as a source of assistance and resources. The Secretary of State,

Condoleeza Rice, refers to these efforts as "clear, hold, and build."[10] Hold is the transitional

period between the short-term imposition of a new security environment and the long-term

establishment of a new social system. It involves passing the control of cleared areas to security

forces, which then protect the long-term effort to reconstruct local social systems. This long-term

effort, in-turn, sustains the local security environment and creates the new political environment

that will ultimately mark the conclusion of the conflict. Creation of a local security force is

---

[9] Department of Defense, United States of America. Cited in Joint Publication 5-00.1, Joint doctrine for Campaign Planning, 25 January 2002, page I-1.

[10] Cited by Julian Borger in *The Guardian*, at http://www.guardian.co.uk/Iraq/Story/ 0,2763,1596197,00.html. This is not a new concept. The challenge has not so much been to apply this concept, but rather how to apportion finite resources among the various efforts.

therefore an action that contributes to a larger campaign of multiple actions over an area and period of time, not a task undertaken in isolation. Efforts in Korea, the Philippines, and Malaya suggest that this process takes several decades.

Local security forces in such efforts range from military units to police. They generally operate in a grey area between police and military roles as militarily weak opponents develop characteristics of both criminal gangs and of military formations.[11] As an example, an enemy may be organized in a loose network of semi-independent gangs that use military weapons and tactics to conduct terror attacks against local populations and reconstruction efforts. They may also sustain themselves with smuggling, black-market, and criminal cash transfer methods. Neither police nor military forces can efficiently combat such an integrated threat. Further, military and police efforts that are usually conducted by separate agencies present problems of unity of command and of political control. The security challenge is thus to operate in both realms, providing a capability that fills the gap between police work and conventional combat.[12] Historically security forces specifically configured for this dual role have taken a variety of forms; one form has been a constabulary. When planning the creation of a constabulary, analysis according to a common set of elements (that are appropriate to the culture and acceptable to the local populace) is critical to this beginning.

---

[11] The reason for this recent trend is debatable, and has appeared in theories such as "Fourth General Warfare," (Hammes, et al) but may simply reflect a Darwinian process of natural selection. Historically, constabularies functioned in societies where there was no local law enforcement due to low population density or simply due to the incomplete advance of a modern society. Recent situations bear some similarities, however this form of threat may be a recent trend precisely because it crosses the border between military and police realms and is thus a technique that is difficult to combat (and therefore desirable, from a practitioner's standpoint) with traditional police and military organizations.

[12] This is not a new situation, in that it resembles situations when local ideologues or would-be leaders and criminal gangs have joined forces to resist a centralized authority. What is new is the scope: improved communications and transportation make this a global rather than regional problem and all threats are only a few hours flying time away from targets of strategic significance; thus "The Global War on Terror."

Analytical Elements of Culture and Constabularies

What is Culture?

Culture is widely discussed in the context of current operations. It is not, however, defined in a way that is commonly accepted or applied for military purposes. Webster defines culture as, "The customary beliefs, social forms, and material traits of a racial, religious, or social group."[13] This is an essentially sociological definition in that it refers to the structure, interaction, and collective behavior of groups. The Department of Defense (DOD), significantly, has no useful doctrinal definition of culture.[14] Key Army doctrinal references either have generally not discussed culture, or have given it cursory mention.[15] This attitude, however, is changing with the rising interest in this topic. The change is illustrated by the recent publication of an "Interim" Field Manual, FMI 3-07.22, *Counterinsurgency Operations*, which defines culture as follows:

> Culture is the ideology of a people or region and defines a people's way of life. A people's culture is reflected in their daily manners and customs. Culture outlines the existing systems of practical ethics, defines what constitutes good and evil, articulates the structures and disciplines that direct daily life, and provides direction to establish patterns of thinking and behavior. Cultural issues include, but are not limited to religion,

---

[13] Webster's New Collegiate Dictionary (1981), s.v. "culture."

[14] *DOD Dictionary of Joint Military Terms* (2001/as amended 31 Aug 05), s.v. "culture. Accessed online on 16 January 2006 at http://www.dtic.mil/doctrine/jel/doddict/index.html. The DOD Dictionary defines culture as "A feature of the terrain that has been constructed by man. Included are such items as roads, buildings, and canals; boundary lines; and, in a broad sense, all names and legends on a map."

[15] FM 3-0, Operations (HQDA: 2001) and FM 100-7, Decisive Force: The Army in Theater Operations (HQDA: 1995) do not mention culture at all, which is not surprising given their focus on large scale generic descriptions of operations. What is surprising is that manuals where culture would seem to be an appropriate topic also fail to discuss it in detail. FM 100-20, Military Operations in Low Intensity Conflict (HQDA: 1990, page 2-3), FM 7-98, Operations in a Low-Intensity Conflict (HQDA: 1992, page 4-21), and FM 3-07, Stability Operations and Support Operations (HQDA: 2002, pages D-2 to D-3) contain only cursory mentions of ideology, politics, and demographics. FM 41-10, Civil Affairs Operations (HQDA: 2000, pages G-28 to G-29) has only a simplistic "bullet list" of factors such as religions, clergy, and how religion affects communication, motivation, socio-economic factors, and politics. Even FM 3-05.401, Civil Affairs Tactics, Techniques, and Procedures (HQDA: 2003, pages 5-19 to 5-20) has only a cursory 1-sentence paragraph on the importance of "cultural awareness," and only occasionally mentions culture in the context of managing interpreters, arranging for food, holding meetings, and conducting negotiations.

political and economic beliefs, tribe, clan, ethnicity, and regional affiliation, military attitudes, and law and justice:

- Religion—beliefs, customs, and protocols.

- Ideology—political and economic beliefs, and work ethic.

- Family—tribe, clan, and family; hierarchies, allegiances, and loyalties; family economic interests; matriarchies versus patriarchies.

- Ethnicity—race, nationality (for example, Arab, Bedouin, and Turkic; Kurd and Armenian; Tibetan, and Chinese; Korean, Mongolian, and Chinese.

- Regional affiliations—Internal to a nation and determine those that extend past national borders.

- Military attitudes—order, weapons, honor, and hunting.

- Law and justice—one system of law or multiple systems; property rights; correction versus punishment. [16]

The "Interim" Army definition is informative because it describes culture in the context of the beliefs, forms, and traits of different groups as well as that of individuals, a topic examined by sociologists and anthropologists. The use of combined sociological and anthropological terminology is important. What is of interest to the military planner is a narrow (and necessarily simplified) examination and analysis of the elements of culture that are critical to the understanding of military operations, their effects, the potential consequences of such effects, and some techniques for analyzing them. [17] The behavior of individuals, such as enemy leaders, key local persons, and potential allies is also of great interest. Such elements are drawn from both

---

[16] Department of the Army, *FMI 3-07.22: Counterinsurgency Operations.* Washington DC, Headquarters, Department of the Army, 2004, pages D-5 through D-6. Interestingly, while "culture" is scattered liberally throughout the text of this manual, appearing 35 times, this is the only specific discussion of it as a separate topic.

[17] While there is a great deal of overlap between anthropology and sociology (most universities combine them into a single department), they differ in technique and focus. Generally, anthropology examines the way culture affects human life and includes sub-topics such as evolution, archaeology, linguistics, and cross-cultural behavior while sociology examines the public aspects of societies and social structures, including sub-topics such as gender roles in societies, family structures, and contemporary social problems. These descriptions are based on the definitions of anthropology and sociology posted by St. Olaf College (http://www.stolaf.edu/depts/sociology/), Hobart and William Smith Colleges (contd next page) (http://academic.hws.edu/anthrosoc/about.asp), Mansfield University (http://admissions mansfield. edu/ps/study/anthsoc.cfm), and Hanover College (http://www hanover.edu/soc/study html).

sociological and anthropological methods. The challenge is to determine what questions to ask and what methods to use to develop them so that they contribute to the overall campaign objective.

What is a Constabulary?

In a stable, modern society, order is maintained by a combination of local police, who enforce the authority of the state and control crime at a tolerable level, and by the voluntary participation of the local population, who (at least implicitly) agree to act according to the social and legal accord that bounds their society. Alternately, in pre-modern societies order is maintained by group consensus, normative standards of "primordial identity" realized by implicit bonds among members and between members and the group.[18] Breakdowns in either society can occur, of course, leading to rebellion or oppression, but essentially the difference is one of scale and the relative formality of the enforcement mechanisms and institutions. There are rules. Everyone understands the rules. Order is enforced within the rules. Collective social units can form and function within those rules. The degree to which this order is effective has been referred to as "penetration." [19] Constabularies are generally not necessary in societies with effective penetration. Constabularies, rather, are created in societies on the border between modern and pre-modern, or where the order system has been disrupted, and where penetration is thus disrupted or incomplete.[20]

---

[18] This is a summation of the thesis advanced by Isaacs, Harold R. in *Idols of the Tribe: Group Identity and Political Change*. Cambridge: Harvard University Press, 1975.

[19] The term "penetration" refers to the thesis advanced by Joseph La Palombara's "Penetration: A Crisis of Government Capacity," published as Chapter 6 in Binder, Leonard (et al) *Crises and Sequences in Political Development*. Princeton: Princeton University Press, 1971, pp 205-232. Palombara suggests that penetration is a product of government capability and of physical infrastructure (such as roads) that enable the extension of physical presence to the various regions claimed by the state.

[20] Extant European constabularies, such as the Spanish Guardia Civil, the Italian Carbinieri, and the French Gendarmerie, were created to deal with serious disruptions of the social order (the Gendarmerie) or during times when state penetration of remote areas was incomplete (The Carbinieri and the Guardia Civil) and have since evolved into national police forces that support effective local law enforcement and the control of national borders.

This is an important point because it defines the political environment in which the constabulary must function. This state of incomplete penetration can be the result of incomplete socio-economic development (an underdeveloped society that has evolved beyond the effective system of pre-modern order) or it could be a devolutionary situation resulting from war, economic or political collapse, or any other massive disruption (such as a post-conflict or post-disaster society.) The result may therefore be a temporary lapse, or it may be a systemic collapse that has eroded a social compact to a Hobbesian world of pervasive distrust and rule by force. In both situations the SRO security task is to impose sufficient order to protect the repair or replacement of the social system. In general a constabulary does this by establishing an intermediate layer between the local military (which concerns itself with large scale external or internal threats that directly challenge the state's survival) and the local police (which concerns itself with control of local crime and culturally-specific aspects such as local social behavior, small scale internal or external threats that disrupt the functioning of society). Constabularies address intermediate threats that, while they do not directly challenge the state (at least initially), undermine the authority of the state and can lead to or perpetuate its collapse.[21]

In order to address these intermediate threats, constabularies are police agencies that are organized and equipped on military lines.[22] "Military lines" generally refer to organization in squads, platoons, companies, and possibly battalions (or their equivalents), with appropriate equipment, training, and rank structure, that allows these units to function as military organizations rather than as ad hoc teams of individual policemen. Given a specific threat, a constabulary may be performing a police function with military means or tactics, or it may be performing a military function with police methods; in either case the culturally-attuned police

---

[21] The description of the constabulary as an "intermediate layer" is conceptual and does not necessarily describe a spatial location. Military, constabulary, and police forces could all act in the same area, oriented on different socio-political "layers" of a complex set of overlapping threats, such as terrorists, criminal gangs, and insurgents.

[22] Webster, op cit.

aspect is what renders it unique from military operations and is of interest to military planners.

The specific form and function of the constabulary is thus dictated by both the environment and

by the culture(s) that form(s) it and in which it operates.

Forms of Constabularies[23]

Militarized Police

These forces are organized to deal with small local threats or bandits. They are typically

company-size or smaller detachments dispersed in small posts. They typically employ military

weapons such as rifles, sub-machineguns, and light machineguns.[24] They may use military ranks

or they may use police ranks, but are generally forces of the Interior Ministry or its equivalent.

They may or may not be mounted or motorized, depending on the local terrain and the need for

tactical mobility. Culturally, they reflect a society with a tradition of anti-militarism or with

suspicion of central authority and serve as a form of regional law enforcement and maintenance

of order that is more acceptable than the use of military units. The "Insular Constabulary" (IC)

established by the US in the Philippine Islands on 18 August 1901 is a good example of such a

force."[25] Officered by former US officers and NCOs (and a few Europeans with military

experience), the IC was organized along military lines, but wore distinct uniforms and used police

---

[23] This paper specifically excludes (for reasons of space and time) "Paramilitary" forces, as defined by the US Department of Defense as "Forces or groups distinct from the regular armed forces of any country, but resembling them in organization, equipment, training, or mission." In function, such forces are generally military-type internal security units lacking law enforcement training or function but which are not under the control of military authority, or are illegitimate, possibly poorly trained, and frequently politicized militias that are not under direct governmental control. This might be an area for some future study. *DOD Dictionary of Military Terms* (as amended through 31 August 2005), s.v "Paramilitary Forces."

[24] One fairly heavily armed example during the Cold War was the West German Border Police (*Bundesgrenzschutz*), which was armed with military weapons reflecting its border security role in the face of a Warsaw Pact military threat. Their weapons ranged up to and included anti-tank rocket launchers, mortars, and flamethrowers.

[25] Hurley, Vic *Jungle Patrol: The Story of the Philippine Constabulary* (New York: E.P. Dutton & Co, 1938) pp 60-61, The Insular Constabulary was unfortunately named: its initials "I.C." in 1901 Army jargon meant "Inspected and Condemned," a term that was commonly stamped on unserviceable materiel or spoiled food scheduled for disposal. The name was later amended to "Philippine Constabulary."

ranks. They were commonly distributed among small district bases from which they conducted regular patrols in support of both military operations and local police.[26]

Domestically Empowered Military Forces

Terrain or enemy strength may dictate the employment of regular military formations to perform quasi-police functions. These may be garrisoned in or near the affected regions, and conduct regular patrols and punitive or preventive military actions as threats appear or attacks occur. They differ from purely military efforts, however, in that they are expected to operate in an environment in which the threat resides among the population, either as infiltrators or as disgruntled or rebellious factions. They may or may not be mounted or motorized, but in general they are organized, trained, and equipped for rapid tactical movement and pursuit operations. Culturally, they reflect a fractured or developing society where there are loose bonds between local and central authorities and where force is carefully modulated but also centralized in order to maintain some degree of control that stops short of inciting open rebellion. The Khyber Rifles, raised in India in 1878 to guard the Khyber Pass (they were eventually employed for other security and military tasks) are a good example of such a force. The British recruited from the local Afghan Afridi tribe, to which they also paid a yearly subsidy for good behavior, essentially "setting a thief to catch a thief." British officers provided the senior and sometimes junior leadership in the organization, while many junior officer and all the NCO positions were filled with Afridis.[27] The Khyber rifles were organized along purely military lines, with military ranks.

---

[26] Ibid, pp 61-65.

[27] Trench, Charles Chenevix *The Frontier Scouts* (Oxford, UK: Oxford University Press, 1986), pp 7-13 and 31. The Khyber Rifles were originally sponsored in 1878 by the famed "Political Agent" Colonel Sir Robert Warburton, and commanded by an Afghan officer in British colonial service, Major Sardar Mohamed Aslam. Initially armed with local *jezail* muskets and wearing local clothing distinguished by red cloth badges, they were eventually regularized with modern weapons and uniforms as the experiment proved successful. While initially very successful, their loyalty was eventually undermined by the Amir of Afghanistan with the result that they were allowed to leave British service at the onset of the 3rd Afghan War in 1919.

They maintained outposts of platoon and company size as a security screen for a larger force which was maintained to conduct punitive raids or counterattacks against any large scale threats or penetrations.

Local Defense Forces

Environments that include a direct threat to dispersed rural populations, whether from physical attack, intimidation, or from political infiltration, require the raising of local self-defense forces. These forces provide round-the-clock protection the local populace and free other forces for patrolling and offensive activities. Self-defense forces live among the population from which they are drawn and may be part-time or full-time in nature. While primarily defensive in nature, they may also conduct limited local patrolling and may occasionally be grouped regionally for larger-scale activities. They are generally ill-suited for roles outside their regions, however, and should not be employed outside their limited local security role. Culturally, they reflect a village or clan-oriented society that is threatened by local bandits or insurgents that exceed the traditional methods of local public safety, possibly a society in collapse or facing an insurgency. A good example of self-defense forces are the Popular Forces (PF) and the larger and better equipped Regional Forces (known collectively as RF/PFs or "Ruff Puffs") of the Vietnam War. The PF were led by local NCOs and officers and were organized as generally immobile village defense platoons. The RF were also led by local NCOs and officers and were organized and equipped as provincial mobile companies to reinforce or relieve the PF when necessary. The RF/PFs were assisted by US Military Advisory Teams (MATs), or as in US Marine Corps Areas of Operation, were grouped with USMC infantry squads into Combined Action Platoons (CAPs).[28]

---

[28] Krepinevich, Andrew F. *The Army and Vietnam* (Baltimore: Johns Hopkins University press, 1986) pp 218-221. Significantly, Krepinevich observes that even though they were frequently misused as adjuncts for conventional forces or commanded by low-quality provincial leaders, had the lowest priority for manpower, were the target of frequent enemy attacks, and were usually equipped with WWII surplus equipment, RF/PF inflicted approximately 30% of all the combat deaths inflicted by Republic of Vietnam Forces on their Viet Cong and North Vietnamese Army adversaries.

What Enables Constabularies to Work?

Methods, Tactics, And Roles

Constabulary forces can function as small military units against bandits or small insurgent cells, but usually use civil police rules of engagement and police methods. Unlike conventional military forces they have the legal authority to make arrests, execute judicial warrants, and control local police when necessary. They can cross internal borders in pursuit. They handle riot control, anti-smuggling activities, border patrol, highway (or other lines of communication) patrol, bandit suppression, assistance of local police, and escort of government officials. For military missions they employ the tactics and equipment common to the local military forces to facilitate interoperability.[29]

While they are police agencies, constabularies are generally organized as small, mobile military units. Their tactics are generally similar to the historic US employment of cavalry on the 19th Century western frontier. Their mobility and communications allow them to overcome weaker enemies by rapid concentration while covering large areas through dispersed actions. Their limited firepower encourages a focus on the collection and dissemination of information rather than on combat. The key tactical principles are mobility equal or superior to their likely opponents and combat power that is superior to likely opponents and also allows for supporting fires between two or more constabulary units. These principles close the gap between the police tactics (individual and small team patrolling) and the firepower-intensive tactics of the conventional military.

These principles apply whether the constabulary forces execute offensive or defensive roles. Defensive roles include tasks such as area defense or defensive patrolling of villages and

---

[29] United States Territorial Government of the Philippines, *Handbook of the Philippine Constabulary* (Publication information not specified, date not specified but estimated from context and cross-reference as 1901; copy available in the rare books collection, Combined Arms Research Library, Fort Leavenworth, KS) pp 1-34.

urban areas that exceed the capability or capacity of any local police. Constabularies may also execute offensive tasks such as offensive patrolling, raids or attacks on bandit or insurgent forces, and riot suppression. They may also develop a special forces-type capability for direct action or raids in SWAT (Special Weapons and Tactics) type special police or police commando formations.

Constabulary units employ fast and flexible mobility in order to conduct pursuit or to concentrate dispersed elements for coordinated efforts. The form of mobility should be suited to the terrain, but should not require specialized military assistance such as tracked recovery vehicles.[30] Depending on the threat, some sort of armored vehicle or aircraft mobility may also be necessary, for special police operations if not necessarily for all units. Any vehicles employed should be carefully considered against the need for the constabulary to operate on the cultural terrain: overtly military vehicles or vehicles that make the occupants seem remote or threatening to a local cultural perspective may alienate the constabulary from the local population.

Constabulary forces depend on integrated local and regional intelligence, particularly human intelligence, and help to bridge the gap between the local police and national military and security planners. Historically police-type forces have acted in an essentially reactive role; planning for short-term threats and responding to crime as it occurs.[31] This is inadequate in an SRO environment engaged with insurgents. Constabulary forces may require military intelligence analysis in addition to their local information-gathering functions: in order to collate information from a wide-variety of sources and means and to project likely threats, actions, and the effects of friendly actions into the mid-term future. This includes not only offensive intelligence but also counter-intelligence and security actions undertaken to protect friendly information. Constabulary

---

[30] In some extremely remote or austere environments mountaineer skills, horses, and mules may be more viable options.
[31] More modern police methods such as community policing and control architecture are more proactive, however the reactive mode and perception of policing is still common.

forces are uniquely suited to human intelligence gathering on the cultural terrain. The combined military and law enforcement capabilities provide information gathering and analysis of criminal and military systems while their local status enables them to operate among the local population.

Historically, constabulary units are smaller than Brigades and lack the staffs necessary for planning and executing multiple and successive actions over extended periods. This limits them to tactical roles, although their defensive role and the security and information effects of their constabulary actions can be a factor in the operational planning of a larger effort. As an example, constabulary headquarters and staffs may be organized along military lines or they may be organized as immobile regional headquarters and staffs, such as the state's ministry of the interior.

Culture dictates the degree of mixture of military and police roles. As the interface between a new or rebuilt centralized authority and the local population, a constabulary acts in a cultural context to manage local perceptions of the legitimacy of the central authority. The key factor is not the military organization but rather the balance of military and police capabilities in a compromise that reflects local culture. Too much force will alienate the populace and too little will make the centralized authority seem impotent or uncaring. Too much emphasis on legality will make the centralized authority seem bureaucratic and ineffective, too little will make it seem arbitrary or brutal. The most important factor is to build or maintain the legitimacy and authority of the state in a way that promotes transition to civil administration and rule of law that are building blocks of a representative government. [32]

This factor requires that the constabulary exemplify the local cultural ideal of the rule of law. As the situation stabilizes the constabulary can serve as the institutional nucleus for new or

---

[32] "Democratic" government implies a fluidity in the political system that may be absent in political systems that are nonetheless representative in the sense that they allow for consensus-based rule derived from some form of representational consultation. An example might be a parliamentary system in which legislators are drawn from tribes, by which they are selected according to informal tribal consensus rather than a political platform.

rebuilt local law enforcement agencies. In order for this evolution to take place the constabulary's actions must be law-abiding and subject to civil authority: the constabulary should be a respected institution that is perceived as fair and disciplined, but also as pervasive in its lawful influence in the local community. In this way the constabulary should be both an example to the local police and a deterrent to criminal or insurgent influence. This influence must be culturally appropriate in order to both maintain the trust of the local population and reinforce the legitimacy of the state it represents.

Systemic Relationships

A constabulary's effectiveness is also a function of its interactions with other elements of the state security, legal, and political organizations. It is subject to the rule of law in a cultural context that must both be locally acceptable and contribute to the establishment of representative government. There are four basic institutional reforms for police (or constabularies) in the restoration or creation of democratic governance. They should be accountable to law rather than to government; they should protect human rights; they should be accountable to people outside their organization and who are specifically designated and empowered to regulate their activity; and they should give top priority to the needs of individual citizens and private groups.[33] Constabularies are thus not primarily concerned with security as a mission, but rather with security as a goal that, along with adherence to these reforms and the achievement of other goals, contributes to the establishment of the rule of law within a legitimate and representative political system.

The integration of a constabulary into a system of state institutions is critically important, and should be carefully planned and executed as a series of interrelated campaign objectives in a

---

[33] Bayley, David H., *Changing the Guard: Developing Democratic Police Abroad.* (New York: Oxford University Press, 2006), pp 19-20. The fourth reform may arguably be limited to local police, if and when they are established.

cultural context. While security forces are often seen as a quick-fix single solution, particularly by states that want to quickly disengage from the distasteful business of counterinsurgency, such forces can come to dominate future efforts in cultures that are not prepared or structured to regulate their actions. Often little thought is given to the tendency, particularly in regions with undeveloped economies and shallow middle classes, for the security apparatus to become either the dominant component of the state or a set of political fiefdoms that simply perpetuate pre-existing social divisions. Constabularies are best when they are embedded in a complex system of the executive, judicial, and legislative institutions of the state which can both support constabulary efforts while simultaneously limiting the constabulary's exercise of power.[34]

Principles, Analysis, and Elements

Principles for Planning Constabularies

It is not enough to consider how constabularies work and the cultural terrain they work on; the planner must also plan for the implications of external intervention, their own cultural biases and how they will affect the local culture. Two principles apply to this planning. The first principle is to assist the local individuals and the constabulary institution in a mentoring relationship. This relationship operates in the explicit understanding that the external agency's ultimate aim is to depart. In departing they should leave behind a constabulary that is not dependent on the handouts and continuous guidance of external agencies. The second is that the representatives of the intervening power should act in a way that is acceptable in the local culture as they develop the constabulary. They should not act in a way that displays condescension or indifference to the constabulary members and their beliefs. The money, expertise, and power that the external agencies wield will have a powerful influence and will tend to create a system of

---

[34] See Bayley, op cit, and Perito, Robert M., *Where is the Lone Ranger When You Need Him? America's Search for a Post-Conflict Stability Force.* Washington DC: United States Institute Of Peace Press, 2004, for a full discussion of this complex issue.

dependence and feelings of inferiority on the part of the locals. This can be exacerbated by

arrogant or indifferent behavior.[35]

Cultural Analysis

As the planner begins to examine the creation of a constabulary in the cultural

environment, there are some anthropological questions that should be answered in order to

understand local culture. These questions are bounded by the specific local circumstances and by

the strategic aims of the intervention.

What is the current security situation? There may be existing security institutions in

place. Such institutions may be corrupt or ineffective, or they may be morally and legally tainted

by past practice to the point that they are part of the security problem. In a worst case scenario,

there may be no security in place and no tradition of such, other than rule by the strong.

Ultimately the creation of a constabulary will take one of three forms: reform or reconstruction of

existing (or past) institutions, an overlay to support existing (or past) local or national institutions,

or the construction of an entirely new system of institutions from the bottom up. Each scenario

carries specific implications of the time, resources, difficulty, and degree of external involvement

necessary to achieve the objective; and each of these implications must be considered according

to the local cultural terrain.

What are they fighting about? Typically, conflicts ultimately derive from the relative

ability of disparate social groups to command resources. This often translates into more prosaic

issues such as fighting over land or some form of portable wealth. Even revenge motives are

generally based in social status; revenge degrades an adversary's status while maximizing the

---

[35]Bayley, op cit, pp 99-100; also author's personal notes. Examples can include paying salaries that are exorbitant by local standards, causing rampant local inflation; it can also include unconscious or unintended consequences of behavior such as female members of aid organizations who wear sleeveless t-shirts as outer garments in conservative Muslim societies, a practice perceptually equivalent to public sexual intercourse in a western context. The intervention will have an effect on the locals, the issue is to avoid giving egregious and avoidable offense while remaining sensitive to how the outsiders and their actions are seen by the locals and the effects that are likely to result.

perpetrator's status. While some small numbers of highly committed individuals or highly

cohesive social minorities may fight for redemptive or millenialist reasons, these motivations may

be ideological rationalizations of more prosaic desires.

What is the local attitude toward corruption? This is a culturally unique perspective.

Corruption may be pervasive; indeed, it may not be seen as corruption, but rather as an acceptable

and common practice. Thus the question is not of whether corruption exists (it almost certainly

does) but rather how much corruption is acceptable given the need for balance between local

social norms and the strategic aims of the intervention. This will most likely take some form of

compromise, but whatever the solution it must ultimately be acceptable to the local populace.[36] If

the intent of the intervention is to create functioning state institutions, then forms of corruption

that circumvent, undermine, or directly challenge those institutions are the most worrisome. The

best time to attempt to confront such corruption is during the period immediately after the

external intervention force has arrived and the local society is still in a state of collapse and

governance is non-existent. If corruption is not controlled immediately at the outset of the

intervention, it may harden into a fixed relationship among local law enforcement and security

agencies. Further, corruption must be repeatedly addressed over time, by oaths that appeal to

local concepts of honor, training on the practical nature of ethics, daily emphasis by advisors and

trainers, and the professional example of US or allied intervention forces.[37] Corruption is not

---

[36] It is philosophically arguable that any human endeavor is not free of corruption. Is tipping a baggage handler in the expectation of better care of one's luggage a form of corruption (bribery)? Is providing a gratuity to a government official in order to expedite an application for a drivers license a form of corruption or merely a gesture of respect given to a person of authority? The question is how much corruption is too much, measured by its effect on the society as a whole and what should and can be done about it.

[37] Greer, James (COL, USA). Interview by author, 5 Feb 06 (part II), Email in author's possession. COL Greer was the Chief of Staff of the Multi-National Security Transition Corps – Iraq (MNSTCI) at the time of the interview; this describes a process in use by that organization at that time. COL Greer also notes the pervasive culture of corruption in Middle East society and the economically and politically damaging effects that result; he goes on to note that while it is tempting to value loyalty or counterinsurgent effectiveness over honesty, in the long run this is a destructive tendency, thus the MNSTCI practice when confronted with corruption (at the time of the interview) was to "... invariably take action and make up the

addressed at the outset, bringing it under control may require decades of international pressure or a subsequent intervention and new start.[38]

What is the basic social unit? Tribal societies will be difficult to penetrate for information, and may resist outside intervention particularly if it inhibits tribal activities such as smuggling. Such cultures may further resent external law enforcement or security agencies if the agencies intrude on tribal independence or custom. Conversely, a tribal culture may welcome a national agency as a neutral arbitrator of local (especially inter-tribal) disputes if it is seen as scrupulously neutral and honest and does not seriously threaten the tribe or its core way of life. An example of a culturally-acceptable neutral institution is the tribal *khassadar* system in Afghanistan.

Tribal motivations may be difficult to discern. Tribes may agree to serve in a constabulary in the expectation that they will be allowed to defend their tribal lands; further they may distrust any other agency in that role. Tribes may decide to support a central government (or to stop opposing it) for a variety of reasons: reacting to insurgent actions that have threatened their livelihood or well-being or carrying out pre-intervention tribal feuds, for example. Understanding the reasons for tribal cooperation is important to understanding the bounds of that cooperation.[39]

In other situations, social organizations may have broken down or been destroyed, resulting in an informal tribalization in the form of gangs and local strongmen. In such situations, forming an institution that will command the loyalty and scrupulous behavior of its members may be very difficult as the locals may have no political tradition of anything other than a large gang.

---

loss of effectiveness over time." Commander Kim Evans, USN, noted from her experience as a PRT commander in Afghanistan that if every Afghan who had every accepted some sort of private payment in the course of his duties was to be fired, there would be no Afghans left in civil service. Evans, Kimberly, op cit.

[38] Bayley, op cit, pp 114-115, describes the situation in Bosnia-Herzegovina, referring to the International Crisis Group's characterization of rule of law in the state as a "disaster," and the United Nations Development Programme's "tremendous effort with minimal results."

[39] Greer, James op cit, Part I (4 Feb 06).

In such a situation the tendency of the institution to Praetorianism[40] may be very strong,

particularly after the departure of the intervention force and before the new state develops the

institutional legitimacy to resist the security services.[41]

What stress is the local culture under? If the local culture is threatened by a perceived

common threat, the constabulary may be able to enter as a protector or restorer of local security

and stability. Conversely, the constabulary must be careful to avoid becoming the common threat

against which the locals unify their efforts. Tribes may themselves be employed as constabularies

against other, less cooperative tribes, while this may offer substantial immediate benefits it may

prove costly in the long run if the strategic aim of the intervention is to build a functioning state.

An example is the Afghan resentment of the Taliban's essentially foreign Salafist doctrinal

enforcement;[42] another is the employment of Iraqi frontier tribes to patrol their own regions

against other tribes or foreign fighters seeking to transit their lands. Iraqi security forces are

currently being organized in multi-ethnic and multi-religious units. The earlier attempts, based in

friendly (or at least cooperative) Shiite and Kurdish militias as well as local defensive units drawn

from local tribes (e.g. the Oil Ministry pipeline security units), are balanced by newer "national"

units drawn from a cross section of Iraq tribal, ethnic, and religious groups.[43]

What are the social trends? The society may be experiencing a period of cultural erosion,

possibly caused by trends such as unprecedented contact with a globalizing culture or possibly as

---

[40] Praetorianism generally refers to the advocacy or practice of military dictatorship. As used here it refers to the tendency for state security institutions to become the de facto or de jure dominant governing apparatus of the state.

[41] An example is Haiti, where the Haitian Gendarmerie gradually subverted and came to dominate a weak Haitian state after the US departure in 1934.

[42] While this was not universal, it was pervasive in western and eastern Afghanistan. Author's notes, interview with Commander Evans, op cit.

[43] Author's notes from lecture presented by COL James Greer, Chief of Staff, Multi-National Security Transition Command-Iraq (MNSTC-I), 14 December, 2005. Quoted by permission of COL Greer. Also, interview with LTC John Nagl, author of *Counterinsurgency Lessons from Malaya and Vietnam: Learning to Eat Soup With a Knife*. Nagl, John A. Interview by author, 2 Feb 2006, Email in author's possession. LTC Nagle draws on his academic research and his operational experience in Iraq to observe that balanced multi-ethnic formations are necessary to the ultimate development of a national identity.

a result of a suddenly deteriorated security or economic environment. Demographic trends, such as rapid population increase, may create a large and underemployed male population. The result is that the authority of stable (e.g. tribal) systems may be undermined without replacement by a culturally acceptable and overarching political model. Attempts to impose such a model may accelerate the trends of change and local cultural erosion. These trends may be unavoidable; the solution may be to mitigate the effects rather than attempting to stop the trends. The role of the constabulary in such a situation is to serve as a tool to mitigate these effects, not suppress the trends. As an example, a constabulary should not be a tool to oppress a large and under-employed male population; it should protect the maturing social infrastructure from violent disruption by radical political movements fueled by such a trend.

How will security actions affect this system? Large, unemployed, young male populations without prospects are ripe for radical ideological penetration, particularly if there is a disaffected educated class to provide leadership and a cultural tradition that engenders violent opposition to the political process. Creating a constabulary is not a panacea. Decreasing national resources, or finite resources facing increasing demand, may lead to smuggling, drug cultivation, or inter-tribal or political faction violence. These, in turn, may accelerate local problems and trends; if not balanced between necessity and reform the constabulary may simply become a praetorian force for regime survival through oppression or it may become a coup force and seek to control the state it was ostensibly created to serve.

What local political leaders currently dominate the security and/or political process? Local acceptance of a constabulary is crucial to its success as a culturally acceptable institution. Identifying the stakeholders in the local areas and convincing them to cooperate is critical. Some political players will be explicitly or implicitly threatened by the external intervention, particularly those who benefit the most from the state of affairs prior to the intervention. These players may be bought off, intimidated, co-opted, provided with a "subsidy" or "pension" to encourage their retirement, or simply eliminated if they continue to resist. In order for the effort to be successful the majority of local cultural players should be induced go along with the intervention force and the institutions it plans to build. Key inducements that must be attuned to the cultural terrain are effective government, respect for human rights, reform, civilian control, representative government, willingness to promote on merit, and the willingness to change specific institutional organization, training, and methods.[44]

Other Analytical Elements

The questions asked after the initial anthropological analysis will vary according to situation, level of analysis, and strategic aim. Generally, planners will seek to understand the security-related sociological elements of the culture at hand, in order to determine the feasibility of security institutions such as constabularies, and the culturally-specific forms they will take. Typical questions will examine the organization of the society and its normal means of conflict resolution; the distribution, source, and legitimacy of power; means and opportunity of socio-economic mobility, and local attitudes toward state-based security institutions. The planner may also examine the likelihood of acceptance of externally-derived institutions: in some circumstances protracted conflict or collapse may have delegitimized previous systems to the point that external intervention may seem a preferable alternative. Some examples of anthropological and sociological analytical questions follow.

What is the local willingness to fight? Some social groups may be more warlike than others and will accordingly be willing to join, assist, or allow their members to join security forces such as constabularies. Others will be less willing; these may be sought for passive support or for agreements to remain neutral and not support insurgent groups.[45]

What is the local cultural norm of conflict resolution? Tribal councils, political organizations, remnants of governmental institutions, or religious orders may provide forms of

---

[44] Adapted from Bayley, op cit., p 120.
[45] Greer, James, op cit, Part I, 4 Feb 06.

neutral arbitration or conflict resolution in the absence of state institutions. These social organizations may, however, have been degraded or corrupted or they may simply be reliant on an environment of local security in order to become functional. Some may have occupied a vacuum since the collapse of a preceding system and are now the only functional order institutions of that society. In such an environment the constabulary may become identified with such organizations as the constabulary is created, with implications for the legitimacy of both the constabulary and the local institution. As an example, in regions where community solidarity has been undermined (by civil war or tribal violence, or by the societal trauma caused by prolonged authoritarian rule) decentralized "community policing" security models, with their reliance on voluntary and proactive involvement by the local public, will probably not work. Alternately, centralized constabularies may have become tainted with the bad reputation of earlier repressive regimes.[46] In tribal societies in particular, there may be an emphasis on the settling of disputes through violence. This can be manifested as widespread fighting, especially among tribes that are well armed or that have access to military weaponry.

In the immediate intervention, external forces can act as neutral mediators in such processes, such as in Herat Province, Afghanistan in the winter of 2004 when the tribal forces of Ismail Khan faced off against the forces of Amanullah Khan; the situation was only defused by the intervention of US Special Forces. Subsequent establishment of a US Provincial Reconstruction Team in this region further stabilized this environment and allowed the establishment of Afghan national forces that would be able to maintain the peace in the future.[47] Construction of a constabulary in a similar fashion, as a neutral (cross-tribal or national) organization of outsiders, could function in a similar way.

---

[46] Ibid. p 93. Bayley cites the failure of community policing in Uganda (in the 1990s) in an environment of crime that reflected tribal conflict, such as livestock theft and disputes over grazing rights and land.

[47] Durham, Hunter R., "Persuasive Diplomacy: Innovative Surgical Operations Maintain Stability in Afghanistan," *Armed Forces Journal*, (February 2005): p 46, also author's interview of CDR Kimberly Evans, USN, former commander of PRT Herat.

What is the local political norm of power distribution between local and regional government? There may not be a tradition of centralized government, it may have been corrupt and ineffective, or it may have been pervasive and authoritarian. In an environment with little or no centralized enforcement tradition, the constabulary may be seen as an intruder unless it operates in a carefully nuanced role as a neutral protector and not as an intrusive force. In an environment with a recent collapse of a powerful centralized state, the constabulary may be seen as the return of an unpopular former agency, or it may be facing expectations of such behavior that are contrary to the development of a rule of law and democratic environment. Warlords may arise in the wake of a state collapse or in lieu of a strong central authority.

Warlords, typically powerful locals who amass their power and retain it through the control of armed bands that operate in the absence of or that can overmatch those of any central or regional authority, should also be taken into account. The term warlord is misleading, however. Generally seen as a pejorative term, the word refers to a wide variety of local leaders who should not be seen as simple caricatures. They may range from bandit chieftains who are motivated by greed and venality and who oppress and harass local populations, to men of heroic local stature who exist in a quasi-feudal relationship with a population that may admire and respect them. Such "heroic" warlords may thus possess great unofficial authority.[48]

What is the local cultural norm of social mobility? In many cultures, military or quasi-military (i.e. constabulary) rank is seen as a dominant form of social status. The constabulary should not displace the development of democratic local institutions. In the North African (predominantly Berber) tradition, the leadership of an armed band is a traditional route to an established place in the local power structure; bandit chiefs and military commanders are thus entry-level positions for aspiring rulers. A variant of this belief system (*baraka* in Middle Eastern and Berber culture) is the Asian model of military success serving as proof of a "Mandate of

---

[48] Author's interview with Commander Kimberly Evans, op cit.

Heaven." Both myths are dangerous to the development of a civil society with subordinate security institutions.

What is the local minority attitude toward the armed security or defense forces? There may be a tradition of local resistance to centralized authority; this is often true in societies in extremely compartmentalized terrain such as Afghanistan or the Philippines. On the other hand, in regions without such compartmentalization the centralized institutions of a state may be regarded with nationalistic pride, particularly in the face of a perceived external threat (as in Iraq). In regions where there has never been effective representative government or where a brutal authoritarian regime has been destroyed, the population may be skeptical not only of the security forces, but of the role of such forces within a representative system that they do not yet feel faith in. The willingness of the population to become engaged with and support local and regional security efforts is absolutely critical, however this population may have no reason to feel such willingness or may even condone such authoritarian practices as torture and summary executions, particularly if the security situation has worsened and the population feels directly threatened.[49]

What social or environmental issues aid or hinder the formation of a constabulary? Constabularies are not merely units, they must be backed by infrastructure that can both sustain them and allow them to evolve over time. Some cultural obstacles include weak political commitment, crime and violence, corruption, dysfunctional administration, authoritarian managerial styles, uneducated personnel, politically subservient judiciary, bureaucratic rivalry between security forces and other military or legal institutions, and a hostile or distrustful population.[50] Infrastructural systems that affect the constabulary include antiquated physical infrastructure; ineffective administrative, financial, training, logistical, and facility management

---

[49] Bayley, op cit., p. 99.
[50] Bayley, ibid, p. 119.

systems; internal review systems and processes, and penal systems. Penal systems, in particular, must reflect cultural attitudes toward both punishment and rehabilitation: they can be linked, if possible, to a national amnesty or re-conciliation program and, possibly, "pseudo-gang" or insurgent/bandit turncoat recruitment.[51]

When the planners begin to consider implementation, one of the key problems will be manpower. Creating stability during SRO is generally manpower intensive. How can the intervention force recruit sufficient personnel while assuring the quality and reliability of the recruits? This problem is made worse when the intervention force is the only legal authority present, whether because the original state has been deposed or was ineffective, or if only because there was not accepted legal state before the intervention. Any recruitment program must take local cultural attitudes and values into account and must reflect the local society in its organization, purpose, and leadership. It is difficult to recruit personnel for and build loyalty to an impersonal force of culturally alien outsiders.

The initial recruitment of security forces may begin as soon as the intervention force arrives in the area of operations. This may take a variety of forms, ranging from the continued operation of local civil police under the auspices of an occupying force to the selective recruitment and vetting of knowledgeable locals as guides, interpreters, contract employees, and security guards. These initial employees may, over time, become the known and vetted nucleus of a larger recruitment and organizational effort.[52] Essentially, once the intervention force has, through trial and error, recruited a nucleus of personnel it can trust, it can then use these

---

[51] The "pseudo gang" system, notably developed and employed in Kenya during the Mau Mau rebellion, is a good example of this, both in its effect as well as in the way it employed cultural beliefs and superstitions to undermine the insurgent organization and membership.

[52] As an example, the first use of Filipinos during the Philippine Insurrection in what became the Philippine Scouts, the Philippine Constabulary, and eventually evolved into the Philippine Armed Forces was the independent decisions of local US commanders to hire Filipinos as guards, scouts, interpreters, and waggoneers; a practice that drew on the earlier US experiences with hiring Scouts during the Indian Wars. See Brian Linn's *The Philippine War: 1899-1902* (Lawrence: University Press of Kansas, 2000) for a detailed discussion.

personnel to recruit more, and so on. Local cultural traits, such as tribal organization, are important during this process. As examples, some tribes may have an interest in working with the intervention force, or it may be possible to employ concepts of collective responsibility by holding the original staff and their tribal organizations responsible for the quality of subsequent recruits. In recent situations in Iraq and Afghanistan the initial hiring of locals has been done with Commanders' Emergency Relief Program (CERP) funds that are committed by US tactical commanders on their own authority. Not only does this quickly establish some local capability, it also allows for the vetting of selected locals over time for a more sustained effort and provides the local economy with employment and an influx of cash during a time of economic disruption or collapse.[53] It is important, however, to bear in mind that even vetted local persons may not be entirely trustworthy, but are rather motivated by interests that are more-or-less parallel with those of the intervening force. Some mistakes will likely be made, the best way to mitigate the effects of which is to maintain a "black list" of untrustworthy people who are not to be hired in order to prevent future embarrassments.[54]

Another issue to consider is the question of from whom does the intervention force recruit? The manpower pool may contain a variety of potential applicants. Former members of security organizations may possess basic or technical skills, but they may also be suspect due to prior corruption, venality, incompetence, abuse, or simply by being prone to authoritarianism or

---

[53] CERP was originally established by Presidential Memorandum and subsequent Fragmentary Orders (FRAGO) in the spring of 2003 to allow for the disbursement of Iraqi funds capture from the enemy. This was later detailed by subsequent FRAGO and ultimately codified in Section 1110 of the Fiscal Year 2004 Defense Supplemental Authorization that was signed into law on 6 November 2003. Martins, Mark S., "The Commanders' Emergency Response Program," Joint Forces Quarterly, Issue 37: 46-52.

[54] Nagl, John A. Interview by author, 2 Feb 2006, Email in author's possession. LTC Nagle cautions that, "… there are no good guys and there are no bad guys – everyone is a shade of grey who acts according to his interests at the time." Also Schnaubelt, Christopher M. PhD. Interview by author, 2 Feb 2006, Email in author's possession. COL Schnaubelt drew on his experience as a staff planner at CJTF-& early in Operation Iraqi Freedom to observe that there was little awareness of tribal issues and connections at the headquarters in 2003, and that a relatively shallow Sunni/Shia distinction was the main focus. He also observed that the vetting process for senior Iraq officers to serve in the new Iraqi forces lacked language, historical, and cultural expertise.

praetorianism. Cultural systems may also be barriers: former tribal warriors or militias may be unruly or difficult to discipline and may retain their original personal loyalties to tribal chiefs or warlords. This process will likely be subject to trial and error; the intervention force should retain hire/fire and disciplinary authority as long as possible in order to affect or replace the culture of the institution through control of its membership and rewards or punishments for certain behavior. Selection of recruitment pools, organization and demographic assignment policies, reward and punishment systems, protective systems (also for family members, possibly in segregated housing), and the links with other local or international/regional security systems will be the keys to this control.

Discipline is critical as a tool for modifying or replacing cultural traits that hinder the strategic aims of the intervention, but it must be in a form that is culturally acceptable to the local populace. Even organizations that have been rebuilt into effective and functional institutions are prone to authoritarianism or praetorianism, especially in the absence of effective and legitimate civil authority. Effective security institutions may become a tool of an authoritarian regime or may become the 'tail that wags the regime dog.' "The foreign policy of developing and reforming police abroad sows dragon's teeth in a double sense: by improving the capability of a major institution of potential repression and by bringing into disrepute the activities of donors both at home and abroad."[55] The global image of the new institution will reflect on the sponsor. While speed may be critical in establishing security, particularly in an environment of eroding or disputed support for the intervention, the intervention force must nonetheless move carefully and deliberately. Speed can be a double-edged sword. It allows the intervention to displace hostile forces and it also allows the imposition of reform models before undesirable local norms can

---

[55] Bayley, op cit. pp 12-13. US security assistance during the mid-twentieth century was so often compromised by such developments that the US Congress abolished the US Agency for International Development's Office of Public Safety in 1974 and acted in 1975 to strictly limit the types and circumstances of such aid in future cases.

undermine such efforts.[56] It also can lead to hurried recruitment and superficial training, resulting in ineffective, abusive, or criminal security forces.

Case Studies

Case Study 1: Haiti, 1915

Introduction

SRO are predicated on the assumption that lasting effects in complex societies can be obtained through the investment of resources and time. Security institutions such as constabularies are a component of such efforts and are often seen as a precursor to other types of SRO efforts, such as infrastructure repair or political reform. The cultural environment in which such efforts are undertaken influences the success or failure of such efforts. The essential optimism that underlies such an effort must be tempered by willingness to not only build security institutions, but also to improve the social institutions and affect the local culture.[57] The US intervention in Haiti is an example of an SRO intervention that succeeded in establishing short-term security through an effective constabulary, but worked with local culture in a negative way to undermine long term institutional stability.

---

[56] This could equate to the creation of effective internal review and judicial systems to offset the tendency to local corruption, such as in Bosnia-Herzegovina, or it may forestall international political pressure, such as occurred during the generally successful, but deliberate and negatively perceived, USMC first battle for the control of Fallujah in 2004. Delay may allow local anti-government actors, whether criminal or insurgent, time to undermine security efforts and shape an information campaign that may undercut campaign objectives.

[57] One often cited example is the Republic of South Korea, which arguably did not evolve a true democratic system and rule of law until the late 1980s. This suggests that such reform might be a generational process, with foreign involvement gradually evolving from SRO, to political, economic, or other forms of support, to serving as a mentor or example of behavior, and finally to functioning as a co-equal partner.

Situation and Environment

The US first intervened in Haiti after a deteriorating Haitian political crisis disintegrated into violence on 27 July 1915.[58] The initial decision to intervene was based on genuine concern for the lives and welfare of US and European residents in Port-au-Prince. The decision to stay was based on two US policies. The first was President Theodore Roosevelt's corollary to the Monroe Doctrine in which he assumed responsibility for the diplomatic and financial behavior of the regional countries. (The intent was to forestall European intervention in the region.)[59] This policy, plus the normal concerns for restoration of order and the safety of US and European lives and property, had resulted in earlier short-term interventions.[60]

These previous US interventions in the Caribbean and Latin America had set a precedent. President Woodrow Wilson (after his election in 1913) went much further than just the restoration of order, protection of US and European lives and property, and the collection of customs duties. Wilson was willing to impose social reforms in the affected states, by military force if necessary.[61] This new policy colored the Haitian intervention, and all the US interventions since.

Synopsis of Events

The Wilsonian doctrine of social reform came into being after the landing of the initial force of US Marines and Sailors in Haiti on 28 July 1915. While the American commander, Rear

---

[58] The Haitian President, Guillaume Sam, was murdered, dismembered, and his body parts paraded through the streets by an angry mob.

[59] Under this policy the US essentially guaranteed European collection of debts, typically by taking over the customs facilities of the state in question and acting as the receiver of its customs dues until the debts had been paid. Strategically, the US was particularly concerned to prevent any potential enemy (which included the major European powers) from gaining a foothold on the approaches to the US-controlled Panama Canal.

[60] Keith B. Bickel , Mars Learning: The Marine Corps Development of Small Wars Doctrine, 1915-1940. Boulder: Westview Press, 2001, pp 52-53.

[61] This was not an entirely new development in US politics: While the US had intervened under strict Rooseveltian limitation in the Dominican Republic in 1905, this ongoing effort was tacitly expanded in 1912 under the administration of President William Taft, when the US Minister recommended direct military takeover of the country to halt ongoing warlordism and widespread corruption. Lester D. Langley, The Banana Wars: United States Intervention in the Caribbean, 1898-1934. Lexington: University of Kentucky Press, 1983, page 115.

Admiral William Caperton, USN, proclaimed that the US intervention would be of short duration,[62] he received more detailed instructions on 10 August that were in keeping with the new policy. Key points were: the US would not recognize a Haitian President incapable of ending the country's strife, and any candidate for the Haitian Presidency would have to accept US control of Haitian customs and finances.[63]

Caperton acted quickly, taking over the remaining Haitian customs houses on 21 August and establishing martial law and censorship of the increasingly anti-US Haitian press on 2 September. When the Haitian President requested the release of government funds, he was told that funds would not be released until the US-Haitian Treaty, specifying US control over Haitian affairs, had been signed and ratified. On 16 September Haitian President Dartiguenave signed and the Chamber of Deputies quickly assented. The Haitian Senate followed on 11 November after Caperton informed them that the US military would remain whether they agreed or not.[64] Among other provisions, the Treaty included a key provision: for the Haitian Government to, "... create without delay an efficient constabulary... composed of native Haitians. This constabulary shall be organized and officered by Americans, appointed by the President of Haiti, upon the nomination by the President of the United States."[65] The US was clearly there to stay and intended to construct an indigenous security force to secure that arrangement. Caperton began by disbanding

---

[62] This was probably not disingenuousness: he had not yet received detailed orders. Ibid, p. 123. Indeed, President Wilson, when confronted by the unexpected emergency and US intervention, only made the fateful decision on 29 July, stating in his instructions to the Secretary of State, Robert Lansing, "There is nothing to do but take the bull by the horns and restore order... and put an end to revolution... In other words, we consider it our duty to insist on constitutional government there, and will, if necessary, if they force us to it as the only way, take charge of elections and see that a real government is erected which we can support." Heinl, Robert D. and Nancy G., *Written in Blood: The Story of the Haitian People, 1492-1971*, Houghton Mifflin (Boston: 1978), cited by Musicant, Ivan, *The Banana Wars*. New York: Macmillan Press, 1990, p. 171.
[63] The US Government policy was drafted and transmitted to Caperton by the then obscure assistant Secretary of the Navy, Franklin Delano Roosevelt. Ibid, p 177.
[64] Ibid, pp 126-129.
[65] Department of State, *State Papers Relating to the Foreign Relations of the United States*, Washington DC, 1915 (as cited in Musicant, op cit, page 202.)

the top heavy, inefficient, and hopelessly corrupt Haitian Army.[66] The next step was to organize a constabulary force as its replacement.

Caperton's efforts ashore were initially carried out by the 1st Marine Expeditionary Brigade under Col Littleton W. T. Waller, a decorated (and controversial) veteran of the Philippine Insurrection who assumed overall command of forces ashore on 13 August.[67] After destroying the few remaining Haitian rebel forces, on 3 December 1915 Waller appointed Lt Col Smedley Butler to command the new Haitian Gendarmerie with the Haitian rank of Major General.[68] With him came a select group of Marines, many drawn by the policy whereby they could hold simultaneous rank in (and draw the US equivalent pay of) the Haitian Army: privates became "Haitian" NCOs, NCOs became junior officers, lieutenants became majors, captains became lieutenant colonels, and so on.[69] Initial recruitment began in September 1915. Eventually Butler commanded a mixed force of 120 Marines in charge of about 2600 Haitians.[70]

Cultural Context

Butler faced a daunting task. There was little on which to build. The Haitian Army had been as corrupt and incompetent as the Haitian state. Recruitment was by press gang. By law Haitian soldiers received pay of about twenty cents per month plus a food allowance; in reality

---

[66] The Haitian Army had a paper strength of 38 infantry regiments, four artillery regiments, four Presidential Guard regiments, and 48 companies of Gendarmerie when the US intervened. It could actually muster about 1000 privates under the command of 308 generals and 50 colonels. Musicant, op cit, p. 202. Caperton's other efforts included other government bureaus such as the Financial Advisor-General, and offices of Public Works, Public Health, and Agriculture. About 250 Americans served as the Financial Advisor and Receiver of Customs, Chief Engineer of Public Works, Chief Sanitary Engineer, Chief of the Gendarmerie (later the Haitian Guard), the Chief Agricultural Engineer, and as their staffs. McCrocklin, James H., *Garde d'Haiti, 1915-1934: Twenty Years of Organization and Training by the United States Marine Corps*. Annapolis: US Naval Institute Press, 1956, pp 42-43.

[67] Musicant, op cit, pp 168-192.

[68] Ibid, pp 184-201. Butler had been recently decorated with the Medal of Honor and had also received a battlefield promotion to Lt Colonel.

[69] Butler credited Waller with sending him the cream of the 1st Marine Expeditionary Brigade, commenting "I have never found their equal anywhere in the United States service." McCrocklin, op cit, p 67. Admittedly, the prospect of receiving pay simultaneously from the USMC, and from the US-controlled Haitian administration (in their nominal Haitian grade) served as an excellent recruiting incentive.

[70] Ibid, p 67.

they generally received nothing as pay was usually stolen by the generals and senior officers. Medical statistics were appalling. 95% of new recruits to the new constabulary (named the Haitian Gendarmerie) suffered from malaria, syphilis, or yaws and 85% had intestinal parasites.[71] There was little infrastructure and the local culture was itself an impediment: facilities were decayed or non-existent, soldiers and officers had little or no training, everyone was hopelessly corrupt and inept, and there was no sense of patriotism or national community. The Marines had to start from scratch.

These problems were solved with time and effort. The real problem was in understanding. Language and culture were ciphers: Butler later commented that he had no knowledge of French or the pidgin Creole spoken by the Haitians. The Americans also reflected the endemic racism of that time.[72] As an example of American attitudes, Col Waller prided himself on his correct and courteous relations with the Haitians and even lectured Butler on the importance of diplomatic relations with the locals. Yet in a private letter to John Lejeune he wrote, "They are real nigger (sic) and no mistake – there are some very fine looking, well educated, polished men here but they are real nigs (sic) beneath the surface. What the people of Norfolk and Portsmouth would say if they saw me bowing and scraping to these coons – I do not know – all the same I do not wish to be outdone in formal politeness."[73] Most Marines of that time, especially the enlisted men and NCOs who formed the NCO and junior officer ranks of the Gendarmerie, were probably more overtly racist.

---

[71] Musicant, op cit, pp 202-203.

[72] Kretchik, Walter E.; Baumann, Robert F.; Fishel, John T. *Invasion, Intervention, Intervasion: A Concise History of the US Army in Operation Uphold Democracy*, Fort Leavenworth: US Army Command & General Staff College Press, 1998, page 8. American racial attitudes provided a de facto confirmation to the lighter-skinned Haitian elites of their feelings of superiority over the darker skinned majority. This attitude even extended to black Americans: Haitians felt superior to the darker skinned black American officials the President Harding later tried to install in Haiti; the result was an all-white American presence which simply confirmed what the Haitians had believed all along.

[73] Hans Schmidt, *The United States Occupation of Haiti, 1915-1934*, Rutgers University Press (New Brunswick: 1971), cited in Lester D. Langley, The Banana Wars: United States Intervention in the Caribbean, 1898-1934. Lexington: University of Kentucky Press, 1983, page 130.

These attitudes were not confined to the Americans: the racism and cultural misunderstanding went both ways. US reform efforts created resentment among Haiti's upper class. American fiscal enforcement cut off the customary looting of public funds. Haitian elites considered American efforts to educate poor Haitians as a dangerous experiment in what the Haitian elites considered a dangerously volatile population. The French-educated elites derided crass and provincial American materialism. One upper class Haitian commented the Americans were "...parvenus in matters of intellect and understanding."[74] Neither American nor Haitian attitudes improved over time. Both sides would suffer throughout the intervention from cultural gaps that doomed some efforts from the start and led to unintended (and undesired) effects in others.

Critical Elements

One of the key cultural factors in the attempt to build lasting Haitian institutions was the political will to maintain the US effort over time. While the proximate motive was provided by the evolved US policy reflected in the Wilson doctrine of 1913, the background for this determination lay in a mixture of beliefs in racial and cultural superiority, a Monroe Doctrine determination to keep the Europeans out, and a lingering horror of the events of 1791 to 1804. US policy makers remembered that the Haitian War of Independence had culminated in the horrific slaughter of what few whites had remained after the French forces had been driven out.[75]

---

[74] Emily Greene Balch, *Occupied Haiti*, Garland Publsihing (New York: 1972) p. 179, cited in Kretchik, et al, op cit, page 9.

[75] Lester Langley refers to the racial hatreds and gears that led to the perception of Haiti as a "pariah" among civilized societies at the dawn of the twentieth century. Langley, op cit, p. 122. For the roots of rising US frustration with the state of affairs, see Ivan Musicant, op cit, pp 158-159. Musicant refers to Haiti's political record. In the first 50 years of Haitian independence, the island state was ruled successively by one king, one emperor, one president, and three presidents-for-life. Then it got worse. Since 1843 there had been 102 civil wars, revolutions, and palace revolts; of 22 heads of state (seven between 1912 and 1915) only one served out his time in office. The US Navy had intervened 28 times by the time Caperton landed his landing force in August of 1915.

US policy makers, then as now, were reluctant to intervene, but were even more reluctant to tolerate the deteriorating crisis near to American shores and strategic interests.

The reluctance to intervene increasingly seemed justified as the intervention continued and pessimism grew. This pessimism derived from the difficulty the Americans experienced as they attempted to advance their various efforts in Haiti. The seemingly Sisyphean difficulty the various US agencies experienced derived from the nature of Haitian culture and the "predatory" society that resulted from it. While Haitian culture is not monolithic or immutable, the sources of Haitian culture are key points when considering any reform efforts. These sources derive from Haiti's unique mix of historical influences: traditional African culture, slavery, a particularly bloody war of independence, the Jacobean influence of the French Revolution, the re-imposition of elite dominance and mass submission, and chronic cycles of tyranny and chaos.[76] One observer comments:

> The upshot has been the development of an elaborate syndrome of destructive/self-destructive political behavior marked by authoritarianism, paternalism, personalism, patronage, nepotism, demagogy, corruption, cynicism, opportunism, racism, incompetence, parasitism, rigidity, intolerance, rivalry, distrust, insecurity, vengeance, intrigue, superstition, volatility, violence, paranoia, xenophobia, exploitation, class hatred, institutional illegitimacy, and mass apathy, aversion, and submission.[77]

The elites who would normally form the backbone of any institutional reform were, in Haiti, the source of much of the problem. Neither Haitian elites nor the Haitian poor had any interest in real reform because their sense of nationhood was severely underdeveloped and limited by a culture that lacked a sense of community. The result was that, apart from very local loyalties, Haitian politics were a zero-sum game to accumulate personal power and to obstruct or destroy

---

[76] Schultz, Donald E. "Whither Haiti," Monograph, The US Army Strategic Studies Institute, 1996, pp 1-2.
[77] Ibid, p 2.

anything that could not be controlled.[78] It was (and to some extents still is) a Hobbesian world in which the strong preyed on the weak and the weak sought only to become strong so that they could prey on others. It was going to take more than just relief work and some institution building to build a lasting and stable Haitian society. Further, some aspects of the American intervention made things worse: the clearly visible military control of civil society undermined efforts to build civil institutions, while American racism simply confirmed the lighter-skinned Haitian elites' racist disregard for their darker-skinned fellow Haitians. The failure to address this culture doomed the Haitian Gendarmerie to its ultimate fate.

Outcome

The Marines achieved notable initial success through regular pay, rations, medical care, and good quality uniforms. These benefits attracted a steady supply of a better class of recruit and as the Marine training eliminated poor performers a sense of sprit began to grow, so that Butler later referred to the "pride" and "swagger" of his Haitian soldiers.[79] Over the next two decades the Gendarmerie continued to improve, carrying out successful small unit patrols, several large unit operations, and some notably daring special missions against rebels.[80] As their military efficiency grew, so did the size of the Gendarmerie and its leadership. By 1922 its ranks included 23 Haitian officers. This number increased to 200 by the end of the occupation in 1934 when the Gendarmerie numbered 3000 soldiers and included companies of light armored cars.[81]

---

[78] Ibid, pp 3-4. This essentially Hobbesian world manifests itself in the extraordinary difficulty in convincing anyone to cooperate for pragmatic ends.

[79] McCrocklin, op cit, pp 66-67. Also Langley, p. 152.

[80] The key factors in this improvement were the personal leadership of the Marines detailed to the organization, the improved standard of combat training and aggressive, morale-building tactics brought back from France by Lt Col Frederic Wise in 1919, and the resultant series of victories over rebel bands which affirmed the Gendarmes' new found sense of esprit. Musicant, op cit, pp 213-234. The Haitians returned the attention and fair treatment with extremely personalized loyalty. One Marine small unit commander commented, "They treated us younger officers… as though we were younger brothers who for some strange reason of inheritance had absolute authority over them. It didn't matter where we told them to go – they went. If we told them to follow – they ran ahead of us, to protect us." Faustin Wirkus, cited by Lanley, op cit, p 152.

[81] Ibid, p 230. The Gendarmerie was renamed the *Garde d'Haiti* in 1928.

Some American practices worked against their success, however. In addition to racist attitudes of many Americans, the drawdown of experienced Marines to other commitments in WWI and Nicaragua exacerbated an already difficult task. The number, experience, and quality of the Marines in Haiti dropped.[82] Brutality by the gendarmes to the Haitian people was apparently condoned. The *corvée*, the 1864 Haitian law authorizing the conscription of unpaid labor for public works projects was revived. The Marines used the *corvée*, which was locally regarded as a form of slavery in a country founded by a slave revolt.[83] Even after the Marines eliminated the practice in 1918, it remained a problem as some unsupervised Haitian gendarmes continued the practice with shackled press-gangs, re-conscription of some discharged workers, and using the labor for private gain. While it was not a general practice, at least one Marine officer knew of such abuse. Marine disregard of summary executions of suspected rebels further exacerbated local resentment and widening the cultural gap. The ensuing investigation and scandal further tarnished the American effort with perceptions that had enormous cultural meaning to the Haitians.[84]

Conclusions

The Marines and their political administration made specific policy choices that, combined with Haitian culture, made their chances of long term success problematic. An example of this was the training of Haitian officers. While significant numbers of Haitian officers were trained and employed (the Marines opened the Haitian École Militaire in 1928), the senior officer

---

[82] Musicant, op cit, p 211.
[83] Langley, op cit, pp 154-155. Admittedly this was done in the face of the extremely limited reconstruction budget available to the Marines and the desperate need for new roads, but while this was even practiced with some forbearance by the Marines (Musicant, p 209, cites one Marine officer who obtained 800 volunteers for such labor simply by providing regular meals and 10-hour work days) the practice inflamed anti-American passions and caused many to flee into the hills where they became ready recruits to rebel groups.
[84] Musicant, op cit, p 211 and 224-225, and 227.

and management was occupied by Americans[85] until 1931; this practice ensured the new Garde d'Haiti would lack experienced staff and senior commanders.

When the Haitian Gendarmerie was added to a corrupt and inexperienced civil administration it was a volatile mixture. While the technical skills of the Haitian officer corps came to be highly regarded by the Marines,[86] their sense of civic duty was their true weakness. The Haitian military the Marines left behind in 1934 was a mixture of police force and army, with a monopoly on organized violence in Haiti. The centralization of communications, transportation, and authority in Port-au-Prince and the disarming of the national population set the stage for the political control of Haiti through the physical control of the capitol. The effective Gendarmerie made it possible for this control to include coercion of the populace. The last element of this mix was the culture as affected by the Marine intervention. Throughout this period it had been abundantly clear that the Haitian state was not in the hands of any civil state, Haitian or otherwise, but in control of the US Marine Corps. "As the only organized armed force in Haiti, the Garde d'Haiti was well situated to pick up where its American mentors left off." The first coup d'etat occurred within ten years of the US departure.[87]

Case Study 2: Morocco, 1900-1919

Introduction

SRO happens for all sorts of reasons. Sometimes, as seen in the Haitian intervention, they happen as a result of an idealistic determination to settle an issue once and for all and, as such, enjoy some measure of popular support and political will. At other times they happen for reasons that are at first poorly defined, these interventions may then take on lives of their own as purposes

---

[85] Kretchik, et al, op cit, p. 12. Haitians made up a majority of the officer corps of the GArde d'Haiti after 1931 (84.6% of junior officers and lower were Haitian, and 40% of District Commanders were as well). Ibid, pp 15-16.

[86] Ibid, p 16. Kretchik cites the competitive entrance exams and instruction patterned after the US Army Infantry School, with the added incorporation of both military and police tactics).

[87] Ibid, p. 16.

and strategic aims are rewritten. These interventions tend to become more complex and more costly. In democracies it is hard to muster political will to continue an effort that is both poorly understood and increasingly costly. Constabularies are a critical component of such efforts as they evolve and expand because a constabulary offers a means to reduce expenditures and make such efforts more self-sufficient. The cultural environment has much to do with the relative success or failure of such efforts. [88]

Situation and Environment

Intervention in Morocco occurred for two reasons. First, it was the last place on the African landmass not yet occupied or colonized by Europeans. (Much of the delay had more to do with squabbling and internal tensions among the European powers than it did with concern over the intervention itself.)[89] Second, the Moroccan state was dysfunctional and the resulting lawlessness was affecting European interests. [90]

Morocco is compartmentalized by mountains into a relatively fertile coastal plain and a series of high plateaus separated by high mountains from the inland desert. It is isolated from the outside world by a dearth of deep natural harbors, and internally by a near complete lack of roads. Moroccan languages, customs, and social organizations are culturally split by this geography and history. The basic cultural division is between Arabs and Berbers. The lowlands are culturally and

---

[88] With that said, national strategic self-interest often fuels even the most idealistic crusade; the Wilson administrations determination to resolve the Haitian situation was fueled, in large part, by a determination to keep out European actors (especially Germany) and to control the approaches to the Panama Canal.

[89] Porch, Douglas, *The Conquest of Morocco*. New York: Fromm International, 1986, pp 138-146. The French trigger to invade Morocco was the resolution of their differences with the British in the Entente (the British got Egypt; France got Morocco in return) and their united determination to keep Germany out.

[90] The British couldn't afford weakness that might invite a German presence; they also were concerned about controlling the sea route (via Suez) to India, while the Spanish feared British domination of both Gibraltar and the opposite shore. The British and French both wanted to keep the Germans out. The French were also convinced (with some reason) that the poorly governed Moroccan territory served as a sanctuary that harbored bandits who regularly raided into Algeria; their worst case scenario was the ignition of a general Algerian uprising from the reservoir of Muslims who lived next to but outside French influence and surveillance. Interestingly, to some extent this presages the events of 1946-1964 and later Moroccan concerns (facing in the other direction) about Polisario. Porch (op cit) describes this over chapters 1, 2, and 10. The implication is that the same problems continue but under new political conditions.

linguistically (if not necessarily ethnically) Arab while the mountainous highlands and inland

plateaus are Berber. The Berbers speak their own language (*Shilha*) and retain some of the

animist beliefs of their ancestors in their local form of Islam. As a result the highland populations

were generally disliked and distrusted by the lowland Arabs.[91]

The Arabs were internally fragmented. Morocco was a state in name only.[92] Nominally

reigned over by a Sultan whose court traveled between the major cities of Fez, Meknes, Rabat,

and Marrakech, the land was divided into areas of poor governance and areas of no governance.

The Berber regions were subject only to the Berber tribal lords who, as in many mountain

cultures, hated and distrusted all outsiders and any neighbors.[93] The dominant cultural attitude of

the lowland Arabs was one of suspicion: suspicion of neighbors, suspicion of other ethnic groups

(the Arabs and Berbers loathed each other; both loathed the few Jews who resided in urban

ghettos), and suspicion of foreigners. (The Arabs feared that foreigners were spies for a foreign

invasion.) Foreign visitors typically had to adopt a culturally acceptable cover story such as

pretending to be a convert to Islam.[94] Europeans typically preferred the Berbers over the Arabs,

regarding the Arabs as lazy and duplicitous, while respecting the more primitive Berbers for their

moral code of bravery, personal honor, and hospitality.[95]

Socially, Morocco was crumbling under the strain of centuries of custom locked in

conflict with modern ideas and reformers. Morocco was politically divided between traditionalists

who felt that the best way to deal with western influence was to ignore it, and a smaller number of

---

[91] ibid, pp 6-8.

[92] Porch, op cit, p 30. The mountains in particular barred the penetration of Europeans from the north and of the nominal Moroccan government from the west.

[93] ibid, p 161. The Moroccans generally acknowledged the spiritual and temporal suzerainty of the Sultan (as opposed to the Ottoman Caliphate), but most declined to obey him in any practical way. The Moroccans called this twilight relationship *bled el-siba* or "land of dissidence." This cultural relationship with centralized authority is a key point in later French attempts to unify the land under a single centralized administration. Porch, ibid, pp 8-9.

[94] ibid, p. 30.

[95] ibid, pp 36-37.

reformers who hoped to create some degree of centralized and modernized state.[96] Most of the reformers, significantly, intended to exploit foreign presence to maximize their own power. Western modern weapons such as modern rifles or artillery could elevate a petty hill chief to a powerful mountain lord.[97] Foreign influence had skewed the economy, devalued the currency, driven commodity prices down, and forced poor villagers into the cities where they came into contact with the culturally alien foreigners, exacerbating tensions.[98] In the cities the *ulama* (Islamic scholars) were the arbitrators of Islamic custom, law, and religion (significantly, to them it was all the same thing).

Synopsis of Events

On 5 August 1907, the French landed on the Moroccan coastline at Casablanca. Unlike previous landings, the French Army had come to stay. The French initially seized Morocco to stabilize their Algerian frontier and forestall German intervention. The situation deteriorated, however, as the French presence caused the weak Moroccan state to collapse. On 16 August Morocco plunged into civil war, when the brother of the Sultan declared himself Sultan in response to the incumbent's failure to effectively resolve the situation with the increasingly unpopular foreigners. The French faced a dilemma: they had landed to secure the Algerian frontier by reducing lawlessness in Morocco, yet their presence had made the situation worse, not better. [99]

---

[96] ibid, page 58.
[97] ibid. pp 161-163.
[98] ibid, p 18.
[99] ibid, pp 150-158. This study will intentionally exclude, for reasons of space, the 1924-1934 struggle against the rebellious Abd el-Krim; the "Rif War," which was essentially a continuation of this struggle albeit with modernist national liberation overtones.

The plan to bring the Sultan under French influence had weakened Morocco.[100] The

French expected to end this quickly and decisively but events proved otherwise. After defending

their initial perimeter against raids, the French began to strike outward from their coastal

perimeter in an attempt to bring the elusive enemy to heel. Early attempts with massed combined

arms formations were unsuccessful, later attempts with fast moving converging columns only

resulted in a series of near disasters as the mounted (and very mobile) Moroccans simply massed

against the most vulnerable columns.[101] Settling in for a long term effort, the French gradually

gained the upper hand by simply grinding the Moroccans into the spring of 1908.[102]

This did not end the French military task; instead it expanded. The French determination

to intervene and their decision to stay once they had done so had much to do with their domestic

cultural and political beliefs, described under the rubric *la mission civilatrice*.[103] The French

acted with the explicit assumption that they were going to improve the lives of the Moroccans.

Since things had become worse, the French would stay until they had made it better. Fascinated

by the local culture but repelled by the incompetence, ignorance, and seemingly random cruelty

they encountered, the French diplomats and soldiers sought to free the Moroccans from their

squalor and oppression.[104]

---

[100] In the initial war the original Sultan, Abd el-Aziz, eventually abdicated under French pressure
and was replaced by his rebellious challenger. The damage was done, however: the French influence (and
perceived dominance) directly undermined the legitimacy of the Sultan, whoever it was, making it that
much easier for rebellious chiefs to gain local support sufficient to challenge whoever sat on the throne.
The original French methodology, "Peaceful penetration" was developing into what cynics referred to as
"Methodical Provocation." ibid, p 147.

[101] ibid, pp 166-173.

[102] The Moroccans obliged the French by only fighting during the day, by persisting in futile
attacks on French squares of infantry supported by rapid-firing field pieces and machineguns, and by
leaving their families and livestock in vulnerable villages that were systematically pillaged and burned by
the French and their native troops. This cultural misunderstanding of ways of war (especially of the effect
of disciplined massed firepower) was summed up by one Moroccan, who exclaimed, "By Allah! We rode
at them as we did when we ate up the Dukellah; but they moved not and before we could wheel round to
ride away to reload our guns, we were right upon them. Yet they feared not, and only a few of us were left
alive to gallop away. Never have I seen such fighting and understand it not." ibid, pp 175-179.

[103] Loosely translated as "the civilizing mission (or imperative)."

[104] Porch, op cit, pp 160-161. French motives were less influenced by economics than the British:
British colonies were sources of commodities and destinations for cheap goods; the French economy,

A new commander brought a more subtle method for the sustained series of campaigns the French waged against subsequent tribal uprisings and local *jihads* over the next seven years. General Hubert Lyautey had already made a name for himself in Indochina and Madagascar; his assignment to Morocco brought his method of "organization on the march," with its accompanying "spot of oil" effect into use as well.[105] These simple concepts, still discussed today, were effective albeit more difficult to implement than the French might have hoped. In the short term, the posts had little effect on the cultural attitudes of local Moroccans who saw no contradiction in obtaining local French medical care or trading with them and raiding them later. Local effects also varied according to French behavior: arrogant French garrisons or French-led indigenous forces alienated those who lived nearest the posts.[106] The immediate task, of establishing and maintaining security, was less problematic: during the period in question the French method generally consisted of fast moving punitive raids called *razzia*.

Security did not solve the French problem. A 1910 French report complained that the state of Moroccan governance was no better than it had been in 1907.[107] There was never a serious military threat to the French presence in Morocco; the French problem was less about winning engagements and more about deterring the sort of activity that was inhibiting the extension of French political influence. Typically military actions would unfold according to a pattern: The rebel force would assemble from a precarious alliance of tribes who distrusted each

---

geared toward high-quality luxury goods and dubious about overseas investment, had less involvement in their colonies. French colonialism was thus animated more by reasons of state, overlaid by cultural idealism, than was the essentially pragmatic and mercantile British approach. Porch, ibid, pp 187-188.

[105] ibid, pp 129-130. "Organization on the March" referred to the combination of military, economic, and political power brought to bear on pacification of a region, over time, through a policy that attracted the populace to stability and economic benefit. "Spot of Oil" (or *tache d'huile*) referred to the effect: a spreading spot of stability which radiated outward from defended points that also served as political and economic centers.

[106] Porch, op cit, pp 184-185. Also Woolman, David S. *Rebels in the Rif.* Stanford: Stanford University Press, 1968, pp 168-169. Woolman notes that the occasional French arrogance was an exception to policy: Lyautey's often quoted injunction (developed in Indochina) was to, "Govern with the Mandarins, not against them. Do not offend a single tradition; do not change a single habit."

[107] Porch, op cit, p 212.

other nearly as much as they disliked the foreign presence. This force would then menace a major

city, often seeking to make its leader the new Sultan. The French would counter with a force

variously made up of the local Army or French forces (frequently Algerian indigenous troops);

the rebel force would be defeated or simply melt away, and order would temporarily be restored.

In this way the French advanced methodically until, by 1912 they had subdued, if not necessarily

pacified, the Moroccan plain. Pressed with constant small scale violence to his rear, Lyautey felt

that the next task was consolidation. His techniques of indirect rule through local *caids* and their

locally raised *harkas* faltered, however; as the French forces marched away, the loyalty of the

caids diminished in direct proportion to the distance of the French forces.[108] Given the weak state

of local forces (and the almost complete lack of any national identity on which to build) long term

stability had became the real problem.

Cultural Context

The solution lay in an understanding and effective organization of tribal societies. French

intelligence did well at broad ethnographic studies of tribes based on their Algerian experience,

although it found itself challenged by the local cultural barrier. The techniques developed in

Algeria worked, but without an established long-term presence and local relationships informants

often gave made-up information or fragmentary reports (in the hopes of a new bribe the next

day). Even French officers who spoke Arabic had their limitations; their classically flavored

speech was often unintelligible to the locals.[109] The local police *mokhaznis* were much more

---

[108] ibid, p. 280. Also, Woolman, op cit, pp 14-15. Woolman quotes the last French Governor-General on Lyautey, "No tribe came to us spontaneously. None gave in without fighting, and some of them not until they had exhausted every means of resistance."

[109] The best results came from the Algerians in French service, who were generally able to get along with the locals.

successful, sometimes simply by having a long gossiping lunch with a prospective informant.[110] This provided a start point. A local constabulary that could establish effective long term presence was the next step.

Critical Elements

Militarily, the French initially faced tribal warriors and *harkas*, feudal levies called up by regional rulers and the Sultan. The French colonial forces initially consisted of Foreign Legionnaires and French units (including, significantly, French units of Algerians). The Moroccan Sultan's forces were notable for their near complete lack of fighting power; their deployment had always been a tool of economic blackmail that descended on the offending province and engaged in rapacious looting and foraging. The French would have to do better, but with the same material. As they gained legal control over the nominal sultanate (in the form of a Protectorate granted by the Great Powers in 1906 at Algeciras) they began to organize their own local units, taking their Algerian experiences as a template. These came in four forms. The *harka* was a tribal levy and was discarded by the French as they began to organize regular units. The *goums* were hired tribal warriors, often Berbers, used for scouting and screening. The *mokhaznis* often Arabs, were police under French leadership. The French also raised regular Moroccan units on the Algerian model, such as *tirailleurs*, *spahis*, and *chausseurs d'Afrique*.[111] While the French did not use the term, of these types the *goums* and *mokhaznis* were in effect a constabulary.

The *mokhaznis* were generally employed to scout after tribal raids and for the garrison of local strong points and villages. While the scouting role was effective, their defensive role generally was not: coming from a warrior society they excelled at tactics that conserved their own

---

[110] ibid, p 187. Porch includes the observation of one contemporary observer that bribes handed out by French officers with only a superficial knowledge of the local culture almost inevitably gave their money to the wrong people, "small men who had no influence."

[111] ibid, p. 64, also Herron, J. S., *Colonial Army Systems of The Netherlands, Great Britain, France, Germany, Portugal, Italy, and Belgium*. Washington DC: The US Government Printing Office, 1901, pp 69-104.

safety, such as scouting, skirmishing, ambush, and raids. They preferred to run in the face of overwhelming power, rather than stand and fight a determined defense; this led to a number of occasions where they simply abandoned their posts, much to the consternation of their French officers.[112] In practice they were generally used as escort and guard details for the French Army equivalent of civil affairs officers (*Bureaux Generale de Reseignment*).[113] They were extremely successful in this role as they enabled the French to penetrate Moroccan Arab society.

The *goums* were externally similar to the *mokhaznis* with the exception that they were typically recruited from Berber tribes who lived along the Algerian and Moroccan borders; the same people the French were increasingly fighting as they pacified the lowlands and moved into the mountains. While this sometimes led to instances of sudden shifts in allegiance (especially if the fight seemed to be going against the French) they were generally loyal if for no other reason than the prospect for material reward was greater in French service than fighting against it. The French were also notably successful in recruiting cooperative tribes to deal with their more troublesome neighbors.[114]

Both units were organized in a similar manner in that they were generally led by French (or Algerian-French) officers and NCOs; over time this began to include Moroccan leaders as well. The initial distribution was one French officer and four French NCOs to a battalion of 550 men.[115] One significant difference from British or US colonial practice was that the French not only mixed their units by leader and led; they also ethnically mixed their regular (i.e. non-tribal) manning over time, filling units with both French colonial and Moroccan recruits, for example.[116] This affected the unit and local culture by imparting a sense of French national identity as the

---

[112] Porch, op cit, p 67.
[113] ibid, p. 129.
[114] ibid, pp 122-123. Porch also notes a later situation where a tribal chief was eventually hunted down by *goum* formations led by three of his sons.
[115] ibid, p 250.
[116] Harris, Walter B., *France, Spain, and the Rif.* New York: Longmans, Green & Co., 1927, page 1823-185. Also Rankin, Reginald, *In Morocco with General d'Amade.* London: John Lane Ltd, 1931, pp 24-25.

units developed internal cohesion and a sense of collective purpose, while discharged soldiers returned to their communities with improved cultural understanding.

Regular pay, given directly to the recruits (to prevent its being siphoned off by corrupt officers) was a key part of maintaining loyalty; not out of gratitude but because the local recruits saw greater long-term benefit in the assured and fairly generous (by local standards) income (and also the opportunities for looting that followed the typically successful French campaigns). While patriotism was an unknown concept, personal honor was a key source of motivation, especially for the Berber tribesmen.[117] Personal loyalty to a specific officer or sergeant in return for fair and consistent treatment was also common: during an abortive mutiny of local units in 1912 many French officers and NCOs survived because their own soldiers sheltered them or escorted them to safety.[118] The benefits of French service became apparent over time; significantly conscription was never necessary: all Moroccans in French service were volunteers.[119] This generally positive attitude, coupled with the cultural mixing that occurred with French recruiting policy, allowed the French military to serve as a tool of cultural modification.

Cultural understanding also allowed some manipulation of local systems to maintain order. As an example in the towns, placing the *ulama* on government stipends (on the condition that they refrain from political activity) helped remove one major source of potential trouble.[120] In dealing with the highlands tribes tribal or clan patronage was the key. Intelligence officers trained in Algeria found they initially knew little of Moroccan tribes but, over time, gained influence as the French presence spread and the benefits of cooperation became known. By

---

[117] Decorations, in particular, had great impact on the tribesmen. Rankin recounts a ceremony in which one *Goum* was decorated with the *Legion d'Honneur*. Rankin, op cit, pp 152-153.

[118] Porch, op cit, pp 244-246. Interestingly this principle was not generally applicable: Porch notes that soldiers who had just escorted their own officer to safety saw nothing contradictory in requesting that another group of soldiers give up "their Christian [for us] to kill." Also significant, the units led by Algerian-French officers and NCOs did not mutiny. The *goums*, recruited from tribes, antagonistic to the mutinous Arabs, and loyal to their source of pay (and anticipating a French victory and looking forward to a little post-victory looting) remained loyal throughout.

[119] Harris, op cit, page 182.

[120] Porch, op cit, p 255.

manipulating tribal leaders who were hungry for more power or resentful of old feuds against their more rebellious neighbors the French were often able to split clans from tribes or divide tribes against themselves. Once done, the French dispensation of legitimacy in the form of recognized civil authority (and delegated local power) as well as government stipends helped maintain this relationship. In this way the local French tribal officer inserted himself into the local culture, gradually becoming the power broker of the modified social order.[121] As time went by even rebellious clans would place one or two sons in the *goums* as a hedge against the future, a cultural practice that the French encouraged, albeit not without some trouble.[122] Generally, though, once a tribe had submitted (and as long as it remained so) its members served loyally.[123]

Outcome

Ultimately the French vision for Morocco was a paternalistic one: happy natives, their conditions materially improved, incorporated into a French political system under enlightened and civilized French colonial administrators. The significant factor was the nature of the intervention, its cost, and how the French managed their efforts in a way that maintained their domestic political will. French colonialism, without the commercial attractions of the British variety, had always been vulnerable to French public and political opinion, notoriously fickle at the best of times. Cost, measured in military commitments, continuous battles, and casualties would undermine the political commitment. The use of Lyautey's methods of native politics and indigenous forces reduced this cost. While Lyautey's system ultimately consisted of the

---

[121] At the national level, Lyautey referred to this as the *Politique des Grande Caids*, a method of ruling indirectly, through co-opted local leaders.

[122] Porch, op cit, pp 273-275. This worked both ways. Placing sons in the *goums* also helped the locals guard against surprise and helped direct the French led force against different tribes or clans.

[123] Harris, op cit, page 182.

manipulation of self-interest and economic warfare waged through the control of the commodities and markets, it worked.[124]

French reforms took a similarly centralized and resource-intensive approach. Extensive construction of roads, harbors, infirmaries, schools, and markets after World War I improved local conditions, but were also controlled and directed by three times as many Frenchmen as the British used to govern India (with 40 times the population).[125] The results were mixed. French pacification (particularly of the troublesome highlands) was not complete until 1934. One author noted (in 1968) that Morocco had never been truly conquered by the Europeans, but only temporarily subdued.[126]

Conclusions

The best the French could probably have hoped for, given the cultural terrain, was to be respected. One French anthropologist, who had served as a junior officer with Lyautey, felt that the French had succeeded by gaining the acquiescence of the social elites of the large towns and cities. According to this, he theorized, Lyautey had reconciled his seemingly intractable problem (reconciling two local populations to control by another, completely alien, culture) by establishing a strong central government that worked through local cultural systems. This system demonstrated its resilience in 1924 when no significant tribes joined the rebellion of Abd el-Krim, next door in Spanish Morocco.[127] French rule was not seriously challenged until after World War II when a nationalist movement arose and adopted tactics of urban terrorism, rioting, and open rebellion. This movement built a political front headed by the Sultan (later King

---

[124] This typically took the form of rewarding the indigenous troops or local informers who gave up rebel food stocks by giving them what they found and allowing them to sell it to the government at inflated prices, which also collapsed the markets of the rebels. Porch, op cit, pp 275-276.

[125] ibid, p 290 and 298; also Woolman, op cit, pp 168-169. Woolman also notes that one port, named Port Lyautey, was named in the French general's honor and is still in use.

[126] Woolman, op cit, p 14.

[127] Woolman, op cit, p 169. Woolman goes on to note that the French intervention against Abd el-Krim was ultimately in order to prevent the establishment of a successful Muslim state between French controlled or dominated Muslim populations in Algeria and Morocco.

Mohammed V) that eventually compelled the French to withdraw in 1956 (to focus their energies on the struggle next door in Algeria).[128]

The Moroccan Royal Army, composed of units originally trained and led by the French, subsequently fought its own (and similarly problematic) struggle against Berber tribes in the Rif region, using many of the constabulary techniques and cultural methods pioneered by the French.[129] In this way, the successful French development of constabularies in this region may be seen as a lasting success. Indeed, during the period of the French Protectorate, the Moroccan units raised and trained by Lyautey were notable for their effectiveness. During World War I, with almost the entire French colonial army withdrawn to fight in France, the French maintained order with adroit use of the *mokhaznis* and *goums*. Moroccan military units that deployed to France were similarly successful; the Moroccan Division was the most decorated unit in the French Army in 1919 and two Moroccan Divisions served honorably in the Free French Army in Italy during World War II.[130]

Conclusion

How Does it Work?

The development of representative government and the role that security institutions, such as Constabulary formations, play within that development are key points to bear in mind. The ultimate success or failure of a Constabulary may be in its role as a servant of the state, as noted in the case of the Haitian Gendarmerie. The Moroccan equivalent, by comparison, has been notably loyal to the Moroccan monarchy as it was to the French colonial administration that created it. Seen in this context, some principles serve as a start point for modern efforts that are also evident in the case studies:

---

[128] Ibid, pp 224-225.
[129] Ibid, p 228.
[130] Harris, op cit, p 182.

-Knowledge of crime and anti-government activity comes primarily from the local populace.

-The worst crimes and security threats can only be solved or interdicted with information supplied from the public that identifies the source.

-Because security forces are limited and cannot be everywhere, the public must take an active role in maintaining order and security.

-The public is more likely to obey the law when the law is fairly applied to them.

-Security force abuse of human rights undermines these common factors and may cause the public to see the security forces as a greater threat than criminals or anti-government forces.[131]

From these principles, some legal and institutional characteristics can also be applied as a start point for modern efforts that is also evident in the case studies:

-The Constabulary must be accountable to law rather than the government.

-The Constabulary must protect and respect human rights, especially those that are critical to a functioning and locally acceptable form of representative government.

-The Constabulary must be accountable to outside agencies who are both legally empowered and capable of investigating and regulating Constabulary activity.

-The Constabulary must give top priority to protecting the rule of law within the nascent state.[132]

Cultural Principles of Constabulary Creation

Some cultural factors that apply to these principles and characteristics become apparent in examination of the case studies. While not all-inclusive, and possibly applicable only in certain limited circumstances and contexts, they depict cultural elements that have been successfully employed.

---

[131] These contextual factors are partly drawn (and modified) from Bayley (op cit) pp 75-78.

[132] Ibid. pp 18-22. These principles are partly drawn (and modified) from Bayley's "Essential Characteristics" for democratic police. Significantly, Bayley's model focuses on the ability to control crime while respecting civil liberties. Bayley sees the respect for civil rights as the dominant factor, noting that "...order is not inherently democratic." This implies that, in Bayley's model at any rate, respect for law is more important than order.

- Culture is not merely important, it cuts both ways. The intervening force must consider the effect of its own biases. The negative effect of American attitudes and policy in early-twentieth century Haiti is a case in point.

- Expert knowledge is critical to success, as demonstrated by the French use of specialist officers. Current practices include the occasional and non-systematic use of experts, such as academics, military faculty, and Foreign Area Officers.[133]

- The effort must be sustained over time – possibly decades – and must evolve as the local system matures. The intervention force should eventually become a guest and partner, not an occupier.

- Good leaders matter. Finding them is a time-consuming process of trial and error.

- Knowing and employing the social bonds of existing groups, when possible, is a more resilient method than attempting to build competing systems.

- Training and organization should be compatible with cultural traits and methods of fighting.

- Regular pay, benefits, and honors must be appropriate to the culture.

- Local forces should be treated equivalent to the intervention force.

- The intervention force must take steps to mitigate the influence of other social groups (e.g. the Moroccan *ulama*).

- Tribal loyalty = the loyalty of tribal members.

- The family/clan/tribe of the members must be protected and see the direct benefit of their association.[134]

Praetorianism

The danger common to constabularies lays not so much in the possibility of failure as it does in the political temptations of success. A constabulary is essentially a military force in organization and outlook, but one with a police department's view of the world. As such the constabulary is likely to be a key player in the internal political makeup of the state. The

---

[133] Trahan, op cit, pp 11-13.

[134] This is a vitally important point. If the intervening force is offering inducements such as economic improvement but the insurgent is threatening to kill the children of anyone who cooperates, then the intervening forces' offer comes off second best. The social group that is being co-opted must feel sufficiently secure to accept the offer. Nagl, John A. Interview by author, 2 Feb 2006, Email in author's possession.

constabulary could become part of a culture of corruption, alternately it could see itself as the only force capable of dealing with (by force) systemic government corruption. It could also become the kingmaker by arbitrating political contests in exchange for favor. For this reason, constabularies must be trusted, carefully screened, and deliberately subordinated to the civil authority.

This can be done by the parallel development of strong alternative and controlling institutions, such as the military, judicial, and legislative systems, as well as allowance for mechanisms of civil control such as review commissions and the civil control of promotions and force structure. Balancing formations among demographic groups or mixing them so that their loyalty is institutionalized can also reduce this tendency. Constabularies may also serve in a protective role, balancing powers to ensure that no other state institution with the nascent state security system has a monopoly on intelligence gathering or the use of force.

The Way Ahead

SRO are rarely seen as wars of national necessity. These operations are murky, lengthy, brutal, and messy and are thus even more politically unpopular than the conventional variety. Operating with, at best, a narrow base of political support, the intervention force must solve a dilemma. It must remain involved over extended time while managing the perception of direct cost[135] in a way that maintains political support for what is ultimately politically unpopular. The practitioner must, therefore, not only fight a foe but also affect the perception that his efforts are unnecessary or that the direct costs outweigh the strategic benefits. This reluctance to engage in such efforts created a modern US military explicitly designed for short-duration campaigns. The US military resembles the armed forces of most democracies in its reluctance to engage directly in such efforts. This reluctance makes creation of security the linchpin affecting the political

---

[135] Casualties, destroyed equipment, etc. Monetary and material supports to a proxy force are easier to justify politically than are the losses to domestic forces.

perception of cost. Effective constabularies give the intervention force someone to whom they can shift direct cost; by making that cost indirect the intervention is made politically viable over the period necessary to bring it to successful conclusion.

Further, in developing a force to which they can shift the direct cost the intervention force also gains a partner who is more effective on the cultural terrain that dominates such operations. As the direct involvement by the intervening force is shifted and as the effectiveness of the security actions improve with local involvement, the direct costs are reduced yet further. In this way the intervening state's dilemma is made soluble. The reduction of the perceived cost makes political support easier to maintain over time and this allows the sustained indirect support that is necessary for success. Further, in the long run the constabulary becomes a regional partner, within the local state but with newly forged cultural ties to the intervening force that fostered it and enabled its success.

Cultural understanding is the critical part of these efforts. Understanding the enemy has always been a military prerequisite. Once it was enough to simply understand how an enemy culture affected the way an enemy army would fight. Today planners must consider in a cultural context how entire societies, including their own, will react to their planned operations. These operations are about building, not destroying. Cultural understanding shapes what is built. Poor or incomplete cultural understanding can hamper even the best executed intervention, resulting in the construction of institutions, such as the Haitian Gendarmerie, that are at best effective only in the short term. At worst they may exacerbate the problems they are intended to resolve, or result in unanticipated problems as the society changes.

All things being equal, effective cultural understanding makes the difference. A poorly executed intervention made with effective cultural understanding at least has the possibility of self-correction and another try; many SRO-like interventions have started badly but corrected over time.[136] A well-executed intervention made with effective understanding can create lasting stability through regional partners with legitimate representative governments that are capable of managing their own futures and that retain durable cultural ties to the intervening power that helped them attain that status.

> The evil that is in the world almost always comes of ignorance, and good intentions may do as much harm as malevolence if they lack understanding.

Albert Camus, *The Plague*

---

[136] The British intervention in 1950s Malaya is a good example.

Bibliography

Allen, Richard F., "The Alabama National Guard in Phenix City – A High Watermark," *Army*, (August 2005): 50-55.

American Psychological Association, *Publication Manual of the American Psychological Association*, 5th Edition. Washington DC: American Psychological Association, 2003.

Azimi, Nassrine; Matt Fuller; and Hiroko Nakayama (Ed.); *Post-Conflict Reconstruction in Japan, Republic of Korea, Vietnam, Cambodia, East Timor, and Afghanistan*. New York and Geneva: United Nations Institute for Technical Research, 2003.

Balfour, Sebastian, *Deadly Embrace: Morocco and the Road to the Spanish Civil War*. Cambridge: Oxford University Press, 2002

Bayley, David H., *Changing the Guard: Developing Democratic Police Abroad*. New York: Oxford University Press, 2006.

Belanger, Tyson F., "The Cooperative Will of War," *Marine Corps Gazette*, (January 2006): 62-64.

Bickel, Keith B., *Mars Learning: The Marine Corps Development of Small Wars Doctrine, 1915-1940*. Boulder: Westview Press, 2001.

Binder, Leonard (et al) *Crises and Sequences in Political Development*. Princeton: Princeton University Press, 1971

Bledsoe, Elizabeth E., "The Use of Culture in Operational Planning," MMAS Thesis, US Army Command & General Staff College, 2005.

Calese, Gary D., "Law Enforcement Methods for Counterinsurgency Operations," MMAS Monograph, US Army Command & General Staff College School of Advanced Military Studies, 2005.

Chandler, Jennifer V., "Why Culture Matters: An Empirically-Based Pre-Deployment Training Program," Masters Thesis, Naval Postgraduate School, 2005.

Charkowske, Kevin M., "Practical Impacts and Effectiveness of Cultural Intelligence," *Marine Corps Gazette,* (October 2005): 20-23.

Cook, Kevin L., "From Scouts to Regulars," *Military History Quarterly*, (Winter 2006): 64-69.

Cook, Weston F. Jr., *The Hundred Years War for Morocco*. Boulder: Westview Press, 1994.

Cordesman, Anthony H., *Iraqi Security Forces: A Strategy for Success*. Westport: Praeger Security International, 2006.

Davidson, Michael L., "Culture and Effects-Based Operations in an Insurgency," MMAS Monograph, US Army Command & General Staff College School of Advanced Military Studies, 2005.

Department of the Army, *FM 31-21: Special Forces Operations*. Washington DC: Headquarters, Department of the Army, 1965.

_____, *FM 31-73: Advisor Handbook for Counterinsurgency*. Washington DC: Headquarters, Department of the Army, 1965.

_____, *FM 90-8: Counterguerrilla Operations*. Washington DC: Headquarters, Department of the Army, 1986.

_____, *FM 100-20: Military Operations in Low Intensity Conflict*. Washington DC: Headquarters, Department of the Army, 1990.

_____, *FM 7-98: Operations in a Low-Intensity Conflict*. Washington DC: Headquarters, Department of the Army, 1992.

_____, *FM 41-10: Civil Affairs Operations*. Washington DC: Headquarters, Department of the Army, 2000.

_____, *FM 3-0: Operations*. Washington DC: Headquarters, Department of the Army, 2001.

_____, *FM 3-07: Stability Operations and Support Operations*. Washington DC: Headquarters, Department of the Army, 2002.

_____, *FM 3-05.401: Civil Affairs Tactics, Techniques, and Procedures*. Washington DC: Headquarters, Department of the Army, 2003.

_____, *FMI 3-07.22: Counterinsurgency Operations*. Washington DC: Headquarters, Department of the Army, 2004.

DiLeonardo, Charles, "Training the Afghan National Army," *Infantry*, (March-April 2005): 28-39.

Dockery, Martin J., *Lost in Translation; Vietnam: A Combat Advisor's Story*. New York: Presidio Press, 2003.

Durham, Hunter R., "Persuasive Diplomacy: Innovative Surgical Operations Maintain Stability in Afghanistan," *Armed Forces Journal*, (February 2005): 44-48.

Elkhamri, Mounir, Lester W. Grau, Laurie King-Irani, Amanda S. Mitchell, and Lenny Tasa-Bennett, "Urban Population Control In a Counterinsurgency," Paper published by the Foreign Military Studies Office (FMSO), Center for Army Lessons Learned (CALL), Fort Leavenworth, KS, 2005.

Evans, Kimberly (Commander, USN). Interview by author, 21 Oct 05, Email in author's possession.

Fallows, James, "Why Iraq Has no Army," *The Atlantic Monthly*, December 2005, 60-77.

Fausti, Robert G., "WHINSEC Tactical Training," *Infantry*, (January-February 2005): 50-51.

Finan, Sandra E., "Social/Cultural Dynamics in the Philippine Counterinsurgency: Considerations for Future Operations," Unpublished Paper submitted to the Department of Joint Military Operations, US Naval War College, 1997.

Gordon, James A., "Cultural Assessments and Campaign Planning," MMAS Monograph, US Army Command & General Staff College School of Advanced Military Studies, 2004.

Greer, James (COL, USA). Interview by author, 4 Feb 06 (part I) and 5 Feb 06 (part II), Email in author's possession.

_____. Discussion with author during Guest Lecture at the US Army School of Advanced Military Studies, 14 Dec 05, notes in author's possession. Quoted by permission.

Harris, Walter B., *France, Spain, and the Rif*. New York: Longmans, Green & Co., 1927.

Herbert, Edwin, *Small Wars and Skirmishes: 1902-1918*. Nottingham: Foundry Books, 2003.

Herron, J. S., *Colonial Army Systems of The Netherlands, Great Britain, France, Germany, Portugal, Italy, and Belgium*. Washington DC: The US Government Printing Office, 1901.

Hobsbawm, Eric, *Bandits*. Revised ed. New York: New Press, 2000.

Hodierne, Robert, "Basic Training: Teaching Iraqis to Fight Like Americans is a Tall Order," *Training and Simulation Journal*, (October 2005): 16-19.

Hoisington, William A., *Lyautey and the French Conquest of Morocco*. New York: St. Martin's Press, 1995.

Hudson, Jeff D. and Steven A. Warman., "Transforming the American Soldier: Educating the Warrior Diplomat," Masters Thesis, Naval Postgraduate School, 2005.

Isaacs, Harold R., *Idols of the Tribe: Group Identity and Political Change*. Cambridge: Harvard University Press, 1975

Iscol, Zachary J. "CAP India," *Marine Corps Gazette*, (January 2006): 55-61.

Jackson, Matthew J., "Swimming With the Natives: Cultural Immersion and its Applications for Naval Special Warfare," Masters Thesis, Naval Postgraduate School, 2004.

Krepinevich, Andrew F., "The Thin Green Line." Background Paper, The Center for Strategic and Budgetary Assessments, 2004.

Kretchik, Walter E.; Baumann, Robert F.; Fishel, John T. *Invasion, Intervention, Intervasion: A Concise History of the US Army in Operation Uphold Democracy*, Fort Leavenworth: US Army Command & General Staff College Press, 1998.

Langley, Lester D., *The Banana Wars: United States Intervention in the Caribbean, 1898-1934*. Lexington: University of Kentucky Press, 1983.

Layton, Robert, *An Introduction to Theory in Anthropology*. Cambridge: Cambridge University Press, 1997.

Leahy, Peter Francis, "Why Did the Strategic Hamlet Program Fail?" MMAS Thesis, US Army Command & General Staff College, 1990.

Lowry, Richard, "What Went Right: How the U.S. Began to Quell the Insurgency in Iraq," *National Review*, 9 May 2005, 29-37.

Marks, Thomas A., "Insurgency in a Time of Terror," Counterterrorism, The Journal of Counterterrorism and Homeland Security International, 11, no. 2 (2005): 46-53.

_____, "At the Frontlines of the GWOT: "Democratic Security" Resists FARC Attacks," *Counterterrorism, The Journal of Counterterrorism and Homeland Security International*, 11, no. 3 (2006): 22-28.

Martin, Zachary D., "By Other Means… You Can't Win a Game of Poker if Your Opponent Insists on Playing Spades," *Marine Corps Gazette*, (September 2005): 68-70.

Martins, Mark S., "The Commanders' Emergency Response Program," *Joint Forces Quarterly*, Issue 37: 46-52.

McCrocklin, James H., *Garde d'Haiti, 1915-1934: Twenty Years of Organization and Training by the United States Marine Corps*. Annapolis: US Naval Institute Press, 1956.

McFarland, Maxie, "Military Cultural Education," *Infantry*, (May-June 2005): 40-45.

Mercer, John, *Spanish Sahara*. London: George Allen & Unwin, Ltd, 1976.

Miller, John Grider, *The Co-Vans: US Marine Advisors in Vietnam*. Annapolis: US Naval Institute Press, 2000.

Mintzburg, Henry, *The Rise and Fall of Strategic Planning*. New York: The Free Press, 1994

Musicant, Ivan, *The Banana Wars*. New York: Macmillan Press, 1990.

Nagl, John A. (LTC, USA) Interview by author, 2 Feb 2006, Email in author's possession.

Noll, Andreas, "How Two Armies Became One," (English Language Version) *Deutsche Welle*, 4 October 2005, retrieved 3 January 2005 from http://www.dw-world.de/dw/article/0,2144,1726674,00.html.

Perito, Robert M., *Where is the Lone Ranger When You Need Him? America's Search for a Post-Conflict Stability Force*. Washington DC: United States Institute Of Peace Press, 2004.

_____, "Hearts & Minds Model?" *Armed Forces Journal*, (December 2005): 44-45.

Perkins, Kenneth J., *Qaids, Captains, and Colons*. New York: Holmes and Meier Publishers, 1981.

Peters, Ralph, "Occupation 101: In Iraq, Pentagon Flunked," *Armed Forces Journal*, (September 2005): 46-47.

Porch, Douglas, *The Conquest of Morocco*. New York: Fromm International, 1986.

_____, "Spain's African Nightmare," *Military History Quarterly*, (Winter 2006): 28-37.

Rankin, Reginald, *In Morocco with General d'Amade*. London: John Lane Ltd, 1931.

Schnaubelt, Christopher M. PhD (COL, ARNGUS). Interview by author, 2 Feb 2006, Email in author's possession.

Schultz, Donald E. "Whither Haiti," Monograph, The US Army Strategic Studies Institute, 1996.

Schwartz, Anthony J., "The Way Out: Iraqi Security Forces," *Proceedings of the US Naval Institute*, (December 2005): 38-41.

Sellers, Priscilla, *Incorporation of Indigenous Forces in Major Theater of War: Advantages, Risks, and Considerations*. Carlisle: The Center for Strategic Leadership, US Army War College, 2004.

Serafino, Nina M. *Policing in Peacekeeping and Related Stability Operations: Problems and Proposed Solutions*. Washington DC: Congressional Research Service, 2004. CRS Report RL32321.

Stone, Michael *Gangbusters*. New York: Doubleday, 2000.

Strader, Kent O., "The Role of the American Advisor," *Armor*, (November-December 2005): 18-22.

_____, "Cultural Understanding... Four Cultural Systems," Unpublished briefing presented at the School of Advanced Military Studies, Fort Leavenworth, KS, September, 2005.

Sullivan, Mike, "From the Ashes: Rebuilding the Iraqi Army," *Armor*, (July-August 2005): 44-47.

Swain, Calvin F., "The Operational Planning Factors of Culture and Religion," Unpublished Paper submitted to the Department of Joint Military Operations, US Naval War College, 2002.

Trahan, James R., "Cultural Analysis: The Need for Improved Methodologies and Doctrine," Unpublished Paper submitted to the Department of Joint Military Operations, US Naval War College, 2002.

Turabian, Kate L. *A Manual for Writers of Term Papers, Theses, and Dissertations*. 6th ed. Chicago: University of Chicago Press, 1996.

United States Marine Corps. *Small Wars Manual*. Reprint. Manhattan: Sunflower University Press, not dated. Original Washington DC: US Government Printing Office, 1940.

_____. *Urban Generic Information Requirements Handbook*. Quantico: Marine Corps Intelligence Activity, 1998.

United States Zone Constabulary, *Trooper's Handbook*. 1st Ed. United States Zone of Occupation, European Theater of Operations: Headquarters, US Zone Constabulary, 1946.

Van Sickle, Jeffrey B., "Stability Operations in Northern Iraq," *Infantry*, (January-February 2005): 25-29.

Weltsch, Michael Duane, "The Future Role of the Combined Action Program," MMAS Thesis, US Army Command & General Staff College, 1991.

Williamson, Curtis L., "On The Ragged Edge: Standing Up the Iraqi Army," *Proceedings of the US Naval Institute*, (January 2006): 53-57.

Woolman, David S. *Rebels in the Rif.* Stanford: Stanford University Press, 1968.

Wunderle, William, "Through the Lens of Cultural Awareness: Planning Requirements in Wielding the Elements of National Power," Unpublished brief presented to the RAND Corporation at the Joint Readiness Training Center, Fort Polk, LA, 2003.